YOUR SECRET WEAPON

Creating the Ultimate Business
and Career Relationship

Best wishes for your continued Career Success!

BYRON G. SABOL

With

Kathleen C. Sabol

Copyright © 2021 Byron G. Sabol
All rights reserved
First Edition

Fulton Books, Inc.
Meadville, PA

Published by Fulton Books 2021

ISBN 978-1-63710-037-0 (paperback)
ISBN 978-1-63710-038-7 (digital)

Printed in the United States of America

My first book, *Success with Difficult People* (Byecap Press), was dedicated to my two loves: my beautiful wife, Joy, and our spectacular daughter, Kathleen. Had it not been for my parents, I would have dedicated this book, again, to Joy and Kathleen.

My parents, however, deserve this one. Thank you both for giving me everything you had to give: your boundless love, your inspiration to achieve, your incredible work ethic, and your commitment to our Roman Catholic faith. I thank God every day that I am the son of George (Bye) Sabol and Kathleen C. Sabol.

Byron G. Sabol
March 2021
Scottsdale, Arizona

CONTENTS

Acknowledgments 7

Prologue 9

Chapter 1: Five Divergent People 13

Chapter 2: Key Concepts 21

Chapter 3: Highest and Best Use 39

Chapter 4: Developing Advocates 47

Chapter 5: Attitude 59

Chapter 6: Knowledge 82

Chapter 7: Mission 93

Chapter 8: Value-Focused 98

Chapter 9: Advisor 110

Chapter 10: Personal 113

Chapter 11: Emotion 115

Parting Thoughts 121

ACKNOWLEDGMENTS

I want to thank those who have contributed to making this book possible.

Let me start with our daughter, Kathleen, for her substantial contributions, including her insightful editing of the manuscript. A special thanks is in order for Pierre Benoit for his detailed (he's a lawyer) review and comments on manuscript content. Pierre is also former mayor of Ottawa, Ontario, Canada. Thank you, Jon McGavin, general manager of the Ritz-Carlton Orlando, Grande Lakes, for providing valuable insight into the extraordinary value the Ritz-Carlton provides its guests.

Others who have provided input to this book for whom I am most appreciative:

Diane R. Becket, PhD	Kyle Hultquist
Adrian D. Bland	Barry C. Olson
Jeannie Bowman	Kathy Richards
Fred Broers	John V. Richardson Jr., PhD
Ruben Carrillo	Joy B. Sabol
Gary Cinnamon	Ken Thorpe
Mary Del Santo	Donald J. VandenBrul
James Hundman	

Thank you one and all!

Byron G. Sabol
Scottsdale, Arizona

PROLOGUE

People who are important to your professional and personal success, such as customers, advisors, business acquaintances, and suppliers, want to feel *good* about their relationship with you. Why is this? Because this relationship is a two-way interaction that is both meaningful and personal—it's about engagement. This type of engagement happens when those individuals feel like they matter to you in ways that go beyond providing goods and services. Meaningful connection occurs when people feel like an individual instead of an insignificant statistic.

When those who are important to your personal and career success become more than a mere acquaintance, they become your advocates. When you have developed the relationship of the advocate, then you can count on that person for a lasting, productive relationship. Even more importantly, when you create an advocate relationship, something very special happens: people will say great things about you when you are not around. And nothing but good can come from that.

Let's embark on creating the exceptional relationships that can change your career and your life for the better by calling to mind Abraham Maslow. We are all familiar with Maslow's theory of the human hierarchy of needs. Right? You're not? Okay, here it is a nutshell: as human beings, we have basic needs that must be met before our higher needs can be addressed. The highest human need, according to Maslow, is for self-actualization—the desire to become the best you can be.

Want to be the best you can be? Why not? Sounds like a reasonable goal. So how is that working out? What are your options for breaking through to a higher level of success? Well, three choices come to mind. Let's see. You can work harder. Ask yourself if you can honestly say that you are already working pretty hard. Are you kind of dogging it at work? My sense is, probably not. Your competition probably works pretty hard too. And by the way, we all face competition. It makes no difference if you work for yourself, for a company, or volunteer your services. We are all selling something—a product, a service, or a point of view to someone—and so does your competition.

Now let's see. You can work longer hours. There's an attractive choice—not! Once again those you compete with can do the same—work longer hours. A third choice is to work smarter. You can acquire new knowledge by going to conferences, take courses, and scroll the Internet for the latest information that may be of help to you. So can your competitors. There is nothing in those three choices that are likely to separate you from the pack.

There is, however, another option. This choice requires you to step outside your mental comfort zone. It requires that you think a bit differently than you normally do. This requires that you take a different course of action. After all, what good is new knowledge if you don't act on it?

The choice I am referring to is this: implement a systematic method that allows you to maximize the value you provide those individuals who are important to your success. Those individuals are your stakeholders, who I identify as anyone who can have a positive or a negative impact on your business, career, or personal goals.

Why do we need to maximize value to other people? I do not believe you can achieve your highest level of career success without having a cadre of individuals who not only value your work skills but who believe in you and who enthusiastically support you. Let me put this another way: to generate the greatest value you can bring to your potential advocates requires that you have access to people who are smarter and more successful than you currently are. This book provides you the tools to do just that.

Most business professionals today miss opportunities to take relationships with key decision makers to a more highly valued level for two reasons: they don't think about it, and they don't know how.

YOUR SECRET WEAPON

I am convinced that the few people who attempt to enhance their business relationships do not take the necessary steps to reach the level which this book explores.

This book is not about just connecting or just collaborating or just thriving with stakeholders. In the pages that follow, you will gain knowledge through a systematic seven-step method for taking relationships to a higher, more meaningful level. These seven steps demonstrate how you can provide a unique, unmatched value to those individuals who impact your life and your career.

When you achieve the relationship level I am talking about, three entities benefit: (1) you, (2) your stakeholders, and (3) your organization. When you create a more highly valued relationship with key individuals, you are making your stakeholders more successful. And when you make your stakeholders more successful, you become more successful. Now let's get started.

CHAPTER 1

Five Divergent People

I want to begin by making reference to five different personalities. The first is a friend of mine who is an architect in Los Angeles. He is a partner in the firm. He's a good technical professional, respected by his peers, and a fun guy to be around. In fact, he's kind of a party animal. But my friend has a quirk. Whenever he gets a call from a certain entity, he immediately responds. He drops what he is doing and answers the call. He has been in important meetings with his partners with money on the table, and when the call comes in for him, he's gone. He readily admits that his behavior has irritated some of the partners on more than one account.

The same behavior happens at home. While having dinner with his family, if the call comes, he walks out the door. You see, the entity that stimulates this reaction has nothing to do with him making more money or advancing his career. The call that stimulates his response is the Make-A-Wish Foundation. When I asked him why he would risk angering his fellow firm partners and his family, I expected a poignant response that would really make me think. Instead, he responded with three words, "I don't know."

Since the years that followed this conversation, I have thought deeply about my friend and his desire to risk professional and personal rewards in order to empathetically serve the Make-A-Wish Foundation.

I think I know why: he likes it! He gets great value from knowing he is helping in some way to ease the pain; to help these deserving kids have a wish that will make their lives a little more enjoyable.

My friend has an *emotional* connection in helping those kids. It's not about monetary success or recognition but because of his emotional bond to the people he serves.

And he is not alone when it comes to experiencing emotion. There are a couple of other people I would like to reference. While you may not recognize his name, you certainly know his company, Starbucks—the largest purveyor of retail coffee in the world. Approaching thirty-five thousand stores worldwide, Starbucks dominates the retail coffee market. And when I say dominates, that is exactly what I mean.

For several years I would walk past the Seattle Coffee Company outlet in Birmingham, United Kingdom. One day, as I walked by, I noticed an empty spot that used to be the Settle Coffee Company location. And who showed up not long after? That's right. Starbucks was now taking on tea-loving United Kingdom.

As Seattle Coffee Company executive, Ally Svenson, so poignantly said, "To a certain extent, we have spent the last three years getting the UK streets warmed up for the arrival of Starbucks."[1] Starbucks has dominated its market through its connection with customers. That connection is based on emotional experiences customers have with each visit to a Starbucks outlet.

Why do people pay $4 or more in some locations for a grande nonfat latte or over $5 for a caramel macchiato at Starbucks? Speaking of Starbucks caramel macchiato, I saw this recently on their website: "Did you know, *macchiato* is an Italian word meaning 'marked'? So a latte macchiato is steamed milk marked with a little expresso." What I think it should say is something like: At Starbucks Macchiato is an Italian word for…marked up 30 percent! But as Pope Francis has said, "Who am I to judge?" This is certainly true for me. Who am I to judge their pricing policies, considering that I visit a Starbucks about five times a week?

Like many successful corporate leaders, Howard Schultz left the company to enjoy some of the fruits of his labor. After an eight-year

---

[1] CNNMONEY. Starbukcs to Roast Europe. April 29, 1998. *Buying Seattle Coffeee, US chain launches sip-by-sip sally into Europe*

YOUR SECRET WEAPON

hiatus, he returned in January 2008 as president and CEO replacing Jim Donald, who took the post in 2005 but was asked to step down after sales slowed in 2007. When he returned, Schultz said, "I didn't come back to save the company. I came back to rekindle the emotion that helped build the company."

You see, Schultz gets it when it comes to emotion. "Starbucks coffee is exceptional, yes, but emotional connection is our true value proposition. I could not believe any more passionately than I already do in the power of emotional connection in the Starbucks Experience. It is the ethos of our culture. Our most original and irreplaceable asset," Schultz emphasizes.[2]

His understanding of the value that emotional connections play in business success may best be found in his remarks regarding marketing when he said, "The art of marketing today is the ability to build this emotional connection. I am not going to tell people where they should be spending their money, but I would advise that all marketing be authentic and relate to reaching into people's hearts to let them know that you want to be part of their life.

"At Starbucks, we have integrated ourselves in a way that is very different than selling a cup of coffee. We have an emotional relationship with our customers. It's not one thing but a lot of things. It's not good enough to have a good ad, but everything you do helps complete the circle…the packaging, the community involvement, the service, all help build that emotional connection."[3] As I said, he gets it.

Let's think about this case study in relation to you. Does the work you do impact the bottom line of your organization? You may not be responsible for generating revenue. You may not be in a formal marketing function or in a sales department, but you are a part of the marketing function. We're all selling something, and you made your first sales call years ago. Think about it. From the moment you are born—the moment you arrive here on this planet—you are calling out for attention. You have just arrived, and you are nothing short of

---

[2]   KNOW Magazine. The spring/summer issue. June 19, 2005.
[3]   KNOW Magazine. The spring/summer issue. June 19, 2005.

a bundle of joy and happiness. Your mother looks at your cute little eyes, and your daddy is so proud as he strokes your tiny little head… and you look at them both with a sparkle in your little eyes…and then…you scream your little head off. You want nourishment. You don't care if your mother is exhausted. That's her problem. You want food! You know what? You just made you first sales call! You incited the emotions of your mother and father to get what you want—food.

As an adult, you may be trying to convince your boss to take an action you want. Maybe you're trying to convince someone to do something on your behalf. We are all in sales, and the emotional connection Schultz talks about is important not just for a coffee business. It's important for every business.

While not a coffee mogul, Marian Kennedy is unique. As an American female lawyer living in Amsterdam, what makes her extraordinary is that she cofounded her own law firm, *Kennedy Van der Laan,* and has grown the law firm to be one of the most successful in Central Europe. When I asked her thoughts regarding the role that emotion has played in her exceptionally successful career, she pointed out, "Empathy, caring—is the essence of living as human beings. I believe we need to touch into the emotional connection, obviously, with our clients and colleagues, but just as obviously with the guy across the table in business negotiations and legal disputes. Only by standing in his shoes and understanding the forces that lead him to act as he does can we bridge the gap and move forward in a positive way."

Marian also gets it when it comes to the importance of emotion in building a business. By understanding the forces that drive the other person, we are better able to make an emotional connection with those who are important to our business and personal success.

Another example of an extraordinary person who understood the role of emotion is St. Theresa of Calcutta. From a young age, she was faced with numerous adversities but overcame these to be an influential leader in her community.

Her father died when she was eight, she left home at age eighteen to join the Sisters of Loreto as a missionary, and sadly, she never again saw her mother or sister. She put aside any interpersonal struggles to respond to the call to serve the destitute and the starving and help the poorest of the poor. For over forty-five years she ministered in her own way to the poor, sick, orphaned, and dying, while guiding the Missionaries of Charity. Why did she make these sacrifices? It gave her great satisfaction. She was her happiest when helping the destitute and the needy.

Mother Teresa has had an emotional connection with thousands of individuals, those whom she has aided and those who have followed her. During Mass at our parish church in Orlando, Florida, medical doctor and member of the Sisters of Charity, Geetha Yeruva, spoke to our congregation. She is cofounder of The Foundation for Children in Need. After Mass, I talked with her about her work and asked her a rhetorical question, "If you were in private practice, you would be making a lot more money, wouldn't you?" The good doctor laughed as she said yes. I then asked her why she does what she does, and she responded, "I want to be like Mother Theresa." You don't want to be like Mother Teresa without having a strong emotional connection to what Mother Teresa accomplished in her life.

The last person I want to refer to is my father, an individual who also understood the value of connecting at a higher level. My dad had little formal education. The fact is, he never finished the fourth grade. He didn't begin to learn the English language until he started school, which was taught by Catholic nuns from Slovakia, and their English had its limits. He never mastered the English language, but he did speak three languages in this order: number 3 was English, number 2 was Slovak, and number 1 was Profane! In spite of those educational and language shortcomings, my dad understood how important making an emotional connection was to our family business.

Our family owned a tavern/restaurant southwest of Chicago. Located in a small town, away from the busy streets of Chicago, people traveled twenty to thirty miles to come to our place. The food wasn't gourmet, but it was good. The drinks weren't exceptional; the gin and tonic tasted like a gin and tonic, and the Michelob Draft tasted like a Michelob Draft. Why did these customers go out of their way when they had numerous bar and restaurant choices closer to home? Because my father connected with them. He would engage them by using storytelling as a tool for connecting with customers. Through his storytelling, customers got to know him on a personal level.

Here are experiences my dad had to call upon: Being raised by immigrant parents who never spoke English. As a guard at Stateville (Joliet) Penitentiary, he was required to be a witness at the execution of three inmates. He was offered the task of being the person to engage the lever for the electric-chair execution of a prisoner. The task paid $50. My dad turned it down. Losing his closest brother in combat in Europe. When I would ask my dad where he got his education, he would answer, "Through the hard knocks of life." Through storytelling, our customers would get to know my father, and my family, on a deeper level.

One of the stories my father told on more than one occasion that patrons enjoyed hearing was how, as a nineteen-year-old bartender on the south side of Chicago, five or six burly men came in one day—not the kind of guys you would want to spend a lot of time with—and they told my dad to step aside as they changed out the beer and liquor over to the new liquor and beer vendor. The new vendor was Al Capone. My dad backed up that experience by giving me a pack of matches that said, "Al Capone's Place," across the front of the matchbook. These unique experiences contributed to my dad's ability to truly connect with those around him.

While each of these individuals—my friend the architect, Howard Schultz, Marian Kennedy, Mother Theresa, and my father— came from diverse backgrounds, each thoroughly understood the role that emotion played in achieving goals. They not only valued people relationships; they created an atmosphere for those relationships to flourish.

Most of us work with others and through other people. This is true whether you work for an employer or are self-employed. It does not matter what type of professional you are: brain surgeon, teacher, or newspaper delivery person. Successful professionals create a competitive advantage for themselves by connecting to their prospects, customers, and stakeholders at a much higher, more significant level.

YOUR SECRET WEAPON

This competitive advantage is achieved through emotional connection, which can create opportunities for you without your knowing about them.

Let me give you a personal experience that occurred early in my career. My first position after MBA school was with Southern California Edison. Following six years of enjoyable work at SCE, I became one of thirty-three candidates to head the largest promotional fund for the Mechanical Construction Trades Industry in North America. The number was reduced to six, and I was one of the six finalists. Each of the six of us was interviewed by the industry's leaders. I got the job. Was I head and shoulders above the other candidates? I doubt it. It just so happened that I was doing post-graduate work part-time at the University of Southern California. After starting my new position, I learned that one of the industry leaders conducting the interviews was a fanatic USC supporter. He had an incredibly strong emotional nexus with USC. What put him over the top to vote for me over the other candidates was my connection with USC. Once he learned that I was attending USC, that was all he needed to hear. That is the power of emotion—creating career opportunities without my knowing about them.

Success in business, career, and in life comes down to this key principle: the larger the number of stakeholders with whom you have an emotional connection, the more money you will make and the faster you will advance your career.

Think about it. The people you care most about, whether it is your spouse, your kids, your parents, or perhaps one or two other special people in your life, you very likely have an emotional connection with them. What about a worthy cause you are committed to supporting? You will do activities for these individuals and causes that you would not do for others.

Now I am not suggesting that the feelings you have for people who are important to your career and business success will equal the level of emotion you have with your loved ones. I am suggesting, however, that there is great value to be gained for your business and your career when you create the higher, more-meaningful relationships that are spelled out in this book.

The ultimate goal of this book is to provide knowledge to help individuals to become the best they can be. In return, they will be devoted to helping *you* become the best *you* can be. This synergistic relationship is achieved when we take our relationships to the higher and more-meaningful emotional level.

So where do we begin? Knowing how to allocate your personal resources is a good place to start. Among your most valuable resources is time. In other words, what is the highest and best use of your time, talent, and energy? Our next chapter will help us answer that question.

CHAPTER 2

Key Concepts

One day, three little frogs are sitting on lily pads, enjoying the tranquility of a sunny day. All of a sudden one frog decides to jump off his lily pad. How many frogs do you think were left sitting on the lily pads? If you answered two, then you are incorrect. The correct answer is that there were three frogs left sitting on lily pads. While only one frog decided to do something, none of the three took the step (or leap) to actually jump off the lily pad. You see, deciding to do something is a thought while jumping is an action taken.

The following action steps that I have created are among the highest and best use of your time, talent, and energy for developing the high-valued relationships we need for greater professional success.

1. *Take responsibility for your relationships.*

Successful professionals, empowered through a positive attitude, don't let valued relationships drift away. People who take responsibility for their relationships remain open to see where the relationships might take them. They are not quick to end a potential beneficial business relationship because their goal is to identify among those who comprise their stakeholders a cadre of candidates to become committed to advancing their business/personal goals.

Your goal is to create the highest level of loyalty among specific stakeholders. This is not "What's in it for me?" but "What's in it for the both of us?" You want them to be a person of influence in your life, and you want to be a person of influence in their life. To be a person of influence in his or her life, you need to take responsibility for that relationship.

Encountering these people of influence can take place just about anywhere. On one of my many flights from Los Angeles to London, I noticed the fellow sitting across the aisle from me was having a problem opening his bag of peanuts. He had a bandage on his finger and was in dire trouble. I asked if I could help him open his bag of peanuts. We started talking, and I asked him where he was going, and he said Armenia. I said, "Armenia," and he said yes, that he travels there one week every year. He was a retired lawyer from Philadelphia, and he does pro-bono work for people in this town. He said they have a street named after him there.

I asked him if he was aware of the Armenian population in Fresno, California. He said he knew it well. I told him I have a sister-in-law who is Armenian in Fresno, and I commented on what great cooks Armenian women are. Here is my point: we are midway over the Atlantic on our way to London, and we are having a conversation about the Armenian population in Fresno, California. After conversing throughout the flight, he later introduced me to his son who is the chairman of a large law firm in Philadelphia. Who knew? This is a connection that wouldn't have developed if I didn't continue communication with a man having trouble opening a bag of peanuts. Remain open to where relationships can take you. And just as important is this: there should always be a next step in that newly founded relationship until you are convinced there is no value in continuing to invest your time and effort in the relationship.

I am amazed at how often I will have clients or prospective clients of my consulting practice who will attend a conference and even sponsor a reception or seminar for prospective customers. After the conference, I'll ask them about their experience and how productive their time there was. Looking back over the years, I've noticed a set of common response to my questions.

Me: *Did you meet some interesting people?*
Client: Oh, yes!
Me: *What did you talk about?*

Client: Well, we talked about business and some other things…what they do…what I do…stuff like that.

Me: *What's the next step?*

Client: (stares blankly) What's the what?

Me: *What's the next step in this relationship you have with the one or two interesting people you met at the event? The event that you or your employer paid for and that you invested time to attend?*

It is not challenging to determine the appropriate next step with developing the relationship. Most important is to find something of value to provide them, such as an article you have read, something you took away from a conference, or offer to introduce them to a colleague where both may benefit. A free Internet source for information that you may want to use is the *Management Tip of the Day* from the *Harvard Business Review*. You can receive one management tip daily in your e-mail. Another free source, Google Alerts, allows you to receive e-mail messages about a subject of your choice.

Taking the responsibility to maintain the relationship also requires you to take the long-term view. I asked a friend of mine who is a partner in a Salt Lake City law firm what the longest time between meeting a person and that person becoming a client was. The answer: eleven years! You may not find the value for yourself immediately, but keep the door open to building relationships, as they will pay dividends down the road.

2. *Create loyalty and word-of-mouth communication.*

Our second key concept is to create loyalty and word-of-mouth communication among stakeholders. A stakeholder is an individual who can have a positive or a negative impact on your career or business life. And just how do we measure "loyalty," and how do we measure "word-of-mouth" communication? By knowing the answer to an all-important question. The answer to this question can drive action you need to take to achieve your business and career success. And here it is: *What do people, particularly your stakeholders, say about you when you are not around?*

It's important to know the answer to this question, particularly when information including stakeholder opinion can be transferred from one person to another anywhere, anytime.

Stakeholders, and particularly prospective clients, want to hear from their peers. They want to know about you and your organization from individuals they know and trust. For example, within a one-week period I was asked by three people for my opinion regarding a particular automotive repair business in Scottsdale, Arizona. Two asked me in a face-to-face conversation. The other person asked me via an online portal. People talk and people listen.

I learned a very important lesson not long ago from a handyman. Anyone who has spent time in Florida between May and September knows that these months are especially hot and humid. Whenever the man who takes care of our lawn is working in our yard in the heat of the day, I often take him a soda. Not long after I hired a handyman to do some work on our property, he was talking with the gardener. Our lawn guy said to the handyman, "The people who live here are nice people." The handyman was telling me this, and then he said to me, "You know, people are always watching you." And he's right. If people, especially your stakeholders, are watching you, what do you think they say about you when you are not around? What do you want them to say about you when they are talking to their friends and their stakeholders?

Knowing what your stakeholders, especially your clients and those important to your career, are saying about you is vital to advancing your business and career objectives. I find it interesting that many professional people just don't get this concept.

In a meeting with two partners of a London law firm, I asked each of them if they ever asked their clients for feedback on the services they provided. The response they gave was an emphatic no. When I asked why they didn't seek client feedback, they replied in unison, "We don't want to hear bad news." This is not the right attitude.

You need to know what people are saying about you. You need to be prepared for feedback—good, bad, or indifferent. Equally important is the fact that you need to act on the feedback your stakeholders give you. For example, I conducted a client-satisfaction interview with a senior in-house lawyer for Bank of America in Phoenix, Arizona. The lawyer provided very meaningful information during our session. I turned over the results of that meeting to my client.

About a year later, I ran into that lawyer as he had moved from the Bank of America to join a law firm. When I asked him what he thought of the client-review experience, he said he thought it was a god idea and that it was meaningful except for one thing. When I asked him what he meant, he replied, "The lawyers at your client firm never acted on the information I provided." Raising the expectation that you will take action on the feedback you receive and not taking that action is just bad business. Don't ask if you are not committed to take action on feedback. Ask the questions, then take appropriate action, and both parties will benefit from the experience.

While it would be nice to be highly valued by all people with whom you have contact, it is not likely—nor is it necessary for that to occur to achieve great success. Knowing how you are viewed can serve as a competitive advantage. But you need to answer the following question: who are your competitors? Your competitors may be individuals who market or sell the same or similar things you market or sell. Your competitors may be colleagues of yours who want the same promotion you want. If you are fighting for budget dollars and someone else is desiring those same dollars, then they are your competition. Whether or not you get that position or whether you get that budget you want will depend, in no small part, on how you are viewed by your stakeholders.

You may think you already know how others view you. You may also be in for a surprise. Look at your past performance reviews. What do they tell you about your performance, attitude, and your ability to relate to others?

A 360-degree review is a good place to start. Most often this type of review will include direct feedback from an employee's subordinates, peers, and supervisor(s), as well as a self-evaluation. It can also include, in some cases, feedback from external sources, such as customers and suppliers or other interested stakeholders.

The results from a 360-degree evaluation are often used by the person receiving the feedback to plan and map specific paths in his or her development. Results are also used by some organizations in making administrative decisions related to pay and promotions.

While a formal 360-degree review would be helpful, it's not really necessary. There is a question you can ask your stakeholders that will shed significant light on not only how they perceive you but how much they value your abilities. Here is the question: "How likely is that you would recommend me to a friend or colleague?" If you are with a business or service, ask a similar question: "How likely is it that you would recommend our firm to a friend or colleague of yours?" The answers to those questions tell you a great deal about what your stakeholder thinks of you and your organization. If your stakeholder is hesitant to recommend you to colleagues or friends, you have a relationship problem. For those stakeholders who respond to this question with, "Highly likely," you need to make it easy for them to do so right then. Technologies exist that allow them to easily post a positive experience with you or, better yet, to post a recommendation of you or your service to their Facebook, LinkedIn connections, and Twitter followers.

When asking that question, intently gauge the person's response. The fact that you are asking that question, as opposed to a neutral third party asking the question, may cause the respondent to be lenient in your favor so as not to offend you in any way. He or she may not feel comfortable telling you something they think you may not want to hear. Therefore, listen intently to not only what they say but how they say it. Ask the question, get the response, and act on the information you receive.

If you want to generate more objective feedback and perhaps create a more-comfortable environment for your stakeholder, have a neutral third party ask questions of your stakeholders about your value. Some people can be reluctant to be the bearer of bad news—news you don't want to hear but news you need to hear.

If you are an employee relying on an annual performance review to get a sense of how your employer values your performance, you may want to consider additional resources. Performance reviews typically are not done often enough and all too often are done poorly, according to David Insler, a senior vice president at New York-based Sibson Consulting. A good performance review gives employees constructive, unbiased feedback on their work. A bad one demonstrates supervisor bias and undermines employee confidence and motivation. The balance does not seem to have tipped yet in favor of the good ones, as Insler estimates that only about 35 percent to 40 percent of companies do performance reviews well.[4]

The annual review's biggest limitation is its emphasis on holding employees accountable for what they did last year at the expense of focusing on improving performance now and in the future. To solve that problem, many organizations are moving to more frequent, development-focused conversations between managers and employees. In fact, traditional performance appraisals have been abandoned by more than one-third of US companies.

Here's another issue to consider regarding performance reviews: people hate performance evaluations. They really do. According to a *survey* of Fortune 1000 companies done by the Corporate Executive Board (CEB), 66 percent of the employees were strongly dissatisfied with the performance evaluations they received in their organizations. More strikingly, 65 percent of the employees believed that performance evaluations were not even relevant to their jobs.[5]

It's not just employees who are unhappy. About 95 percent of managers say they aren't satisfied with their organization's performance management processes either, and 90 percent of HR professionals don't believe their company's performance reviews provide accurate information, CEB researchers found.[6]

Frequency of the performance review is clearly an issue. At most places, says Peter Cappelli, head of Wharton's Center for Human Resources, reviews occur annually. "If you wait a year to tell employ-

---

[4] "Should Performance Reviews Be Fired?" Knowledge@Wharton (University of Pennsylvania). April 27, 2011.

[5] Jinsoek Chun, Joel Brockner and David De Cremer. "People Don't Want to Be Compared with Others in Performance Reviews. They Want to Be Compared with Themselves." HBR. March 22, 2018.

[6] Knowledge@Wharton (University of Pennsylvania) April 27, 2011.

ees how they are doing, they are almost always surprised and unhappy if the results are not positive." Every employee wants to know how he or she is doing. Individuals responsible for giving performance reviews need to realize that certain employees need formal feedback more than once a year.[7]

Even if the annual performance review system that you experience is not flawed, keep in mind that the annual review is a one-time assessment delivered to you on one of 365 days throughout the year. There are 364 other days throughout the year where you can impact others. It's easy to go about doing your job, completing your responsibilities, and to assume that your employer (or your client) agrees that you are you are doing well. You need to know how you are perceived. Here's my point: don't wait for your annual performance review to be the primary measure of your value to your organization or to your clients. Seek feedback regularly—face-to-face, especially at the end of projects—to gain a more-consistent flow of quality information regarding your perceived value. That feedback will provide value for you not only now but in the years to come.

3. *Mentorship.*

The year 2020 has proven to create great stress and uncertainty in the communities in which we work and live. Planning one's career and seeking opportunities for advancement is challenging enough in the best of times, let alone doing so during an international pandemic. Now is the time to consider tapping into a significant career resource: mentorship.

Mentors can serve as a very valuable resource not only by providing you with objective feedback but also in assisting you to achieve your career objectives. If your career objective includes generating more income, securing new career opportunities, or general career management, a mentor can help.

A mentor relationship has proven quite valuable for some highly successful professional. Steve Jobs, cofounder of Apple, Inc.; Mark

---

[7] Knowledge@Wharton (University of Pennsylvania). April 27, 2011.

YOUR SECRET WEAPON

Zuckerberg, cofounder of Facebook, Inc.; Bill Gates, cofounder of the world's largest software business, Microsoft; and Jeff Bezos, founder of Amazon and currently the world's richest person, had a few things in common. Among them: high IQ, exceptional entrepreneurial instincts, and a mentor. Steve Jobs and Jeff Bezos had Bill Campbell as a mentor, Mark Zuckerberg had Steve Jobs as a mentor, and Bill Gates had Warren Buffett as his mentor. What does that tell you? If these icons recognize the value of having a mentor, perhaps you might also benefit from a mentor.

Mentoring has been shown to have a positive effect on one's career. A study by Gerard Roche found that of the 63.5 percent of the 1,250 respondents who had a mentor (defined as "a person who took a personal interest in your career and who guided or sponsored you") were on the average better paid (they average $118,900 in total cash compensation, somewhat more than the $114,200 of those who had no mentor), reached their positions faster, and were more satisfied with their work and careers than their non-mentored counterparts. They also averaged higher percentage gains in salary, bonus, and total compensation than executives who did not have a mentor.[8]

While the concept of mentoring has changed over the years, the need for career counseling has not. In fact, because most careers take numerous twists and turns in today's world, it's required more than ever. Because the world moves fast and people change jobs and careers more often, a long-term advising relationship may not be necessary. Nor does a mentoring session need be some long, structured session. Your mentoring time can be short and to the point. The advice and guidance may be richer and more relevant if it comes from someone who knows you well and understands your goals. You still need to build relationships so that when you desire advice, you have the connections in place. A mentor should be at the center of those relationships.

Ideally, you have at least one mentor and, better yet, two mentors: one mentor in your organization you can turn to for valuable insights to weave your way through the political maze and other

---

[8] HBR 1979: Research by Gerard Roche, former senior chairman of the recruiting firm, Heidrick & Struggles.

challenges you face inside the organization; the other mentor should come from outside of your company or organization who can provide an objective view for you.

The key is to find the right kind of advice from the right person at the right time.

Knowing what makes for a good mentor can assist you to identify that person who can fill the mentor role. John V. Richardson Jr., PhD, has provided the following in an answer to what makes a good mentor:

A cursory review of the literature suggests a variety of answers such as "a satisfied mentee;" "a strong sense of self;" "a good listener;" someone "offering support, encouragement, and listening;" "a person who is willing to share of themselves;" "mentors try to unite the head and the heart;" "shares knowledge and wisdom and draws out the possibilities;" "its vision, voice, and vocation—building a relationship;" or "someone who can offer advice to me on issues besides academic matters."

However, I have found one of the best summaries:

Many people feel that being a mentor requires special skills, but mentors are simply people who have the qualities of good role models. The table below provides valuable information for you to evaluate your own journey with a mentor.

Mentors listen.	They maintain eye contact and give mentees their full attention.
Mentors guide.	Mentors are there to help their mentees find life direction, never to push them.
Mentors are practical.	They give insights about keeping on task and setting goals and priorities.
Mentors educate.	Mentors educate about life and their own careers.
Mentors provide insight.	Mentors use their personal experience to help their mentees avoid mistakes and learn from good decisions.

YOUR SECRET WEAPON

Mentors are accessible.	Mentors are available as a resource and a sounding board.
Mentors criticize constructively.	When necessary, mentors point out areas that need improvement, always focusing on the mentee's behavior, never his/her character.
Mentors are supportive.	No matter how painful the mentee's experience, mentors continue to encourage them to learn and improve.
Mentors are specific.	Mentors give specific advice on what was done well or could be corrected, what was achieved and the benefits of various actions.
Mentors care.	Mentors care about their mentee's progress in school and career planning, as well as their personal development.
Mentors succeed.	Mentors not only are successful themselves but they also foster success in others.
Mentors are admirable.	Mentors are usually well respected in their organizations and in the community.

Courtesy: The Connecticut Mentoring Partnership and
the Business and Legal Reports, Inc.—Best Practices in
Human Resources, Issue 653, September 30, 1999.[9]

Compiled: John V. Richardson Jr., UCLA Professor
Emeritus of Information Studies and Adjunct Professor,
Charles Sturt University, NSW (AY 2016-2018)

---

[9] *Courtesy:* The Connecticut Mentoring Partnership and the Business and Legal Reports, Inc. "*Best Practices in Human Resources.*" Issue 653. September 30, 1999. *Compiled:* John V. Richardson Jr., UCLA Professor Emeritus of Information Studies and Adjunct Professor, Charles Sturt University, NSW (AY 2016–2018).

4. *Think 98/2*

Somewhere in your education—formal or otherwise—you may have heard of the 80/20 principle. If not, here's a brief summary. In 1897 the French economist Alfredo Pareto observed that 20 percent of the factors in most situations account for 80 percent of what happens. His discovery has since been called many names, including the Pareto principle, the Pareto law, the 80/20 rule, the principle of least effort, and the principle of imbalance. Among principles of the 80/20 Rule are the following:

- 80 percent of a company's profits come from 20 percent of its customers.
- 80 percent of a company's sales are made by 20 percent of its sales staff.
- 80 percent of your production will come from 20 percent of your staff.

Pareto's principle, the 80/20 rule, should serve as a daily reminder to focus 80 percent of your time and energy on the 20 percent of your work that is really important. Don't just "work smart." Work smart on the right things.

If the value of the Pareto Principle is that it reminds one to focus on the 20 percent that matters, then what might we accomplish if we refocus our percentages? A number greater than 80 percent of your career and your business success will be determined by a far-smaller number than 20 percent of individuals important to you. It's time to refocus Pareto's 80/20 rule!

Instead of the 80/20 rule, I strongly recommend that you think: 98/2! I am convinced that *two percent* of the individuals in your life will determine your career and your business success. These 2 percent are the audience in your career and life performance. When you retire and leave the stage of the workplace and as the curtain is coming down on your career, these 2 percent are the audience members upon whom—hopefully—you will have focused your time, talent, and energy.

YOUR SECRET WEAPON

These 2 percent influence how much money you will make in your career. They influence the size of your office, and they impact the value of your retirement package.

Your choice of individuals with whom you invest your valuable time and energy is extremely vital. A small number of alliances, the 2 percent, will account for a large proportion of your relationship value. With that in mind, let's turn our attention to creating an "A" team.

Everyone agrees that relationships are important for career and business success, and one of the key skills for building critical business relationships is thinking strategically about who is worth knowing. Time constraints, current career responsibilities, and unexpected occurrences necessitate a selective approach. Strategic relationship-building means pragmatically identifying a small set of people who are in influential positions and whose help could advance your career and business interests. This is not about forming friendships; although new friendships may result. This is about dispassionately getting close to people who can help you advance your career and achieve business success.

You cannot achieve your highest level of career success without having a cadre of individuals who value your work skills, believe in you, and are willing to support you. Highly successful people don't go it alone.

I am reminded of a breakfast meeting in Los Angeles with a partner from McKinsey & Company. As we chatted, he asked me if I knew a particular partner in one of the top law firms based in Los Angeles. I knew him, but I didn't mention that the lawyer was a principal in hiring me at that law firm. The McKinsey partner said, "He works hard, doesn't he?" I responded, "Yes, in fact, he's one of the first in the office in the morning and one of the last to leave in the evening." The McKinsey partner then said, "He doesn't have a franchise. He takes all of the responsibility for developing his book of business on his own shoulders. He doesn't have a support system to refer him business or help sell him to prospects. We don't do that at McKinsey. We don't want any one person at McKinsey to be solely responsible for producing business. We share that load."

McKinsey calls it a franchise. I prefer to call it an "A" team. An "A" team is comprised of individuals who share common business and career interests and who are focused on helping each other reach his or her goals. They are not all superiors, subordinates, or even peers. They are the people who can best get the job done—whether it consists of securing an assignment or carrying it out.

According to Brian Uzzi and Shannon Dunlap, as published in the *Harvard Business Review*, when we make judgments, we use both public and private information. Public information is easily available from a variety of sources, including the Internet, but precisely because it is so public and easily available it offers significantly less competitive advantage than it once did.[10]

One of the greatest benefits of having an "A" team is the potential it represents for having access to private information. By private information, I am certainly not referring to any illegal insider trading information—nonpublic facts regarding the plans or conditions of a publicly traded company that could provide a financial advantage when used to buy or sell shares of that or another company's securities.

The private information I am referring to is gathered from personal contacts who can offer insights, data, and details that cannot be found in the public domain. These include a forthcoming board opening that you may want to pursue, the release date of a new product, unpublished software code, or knowledge about what a particular interviewer is looking for in candidates. Private information can give you an edge, though it is more subjective than public information because usually it is not verified by an independent party, such as Dun & Bradstreet.

The value of your private information to others—and the value of others' private information to you—depends on how much trust exists in the network of your relationships. By creating trust among

---

[10] HBR. December 2005. "How to Build Your Network" by Brian Uzzi and Shannon Dunlap. Brian Uzzi is the Richard L. Thomas Professor of Leadership and Organizational Change at Northwestern's Kellogg School of Management and the codirector of the Northwestern Institute on Complex Systems (NICO). Shannon Dunlap is a journalist and writer based in New York City.

YOUR SECRET WEAPON

your "A" team members, you position yourself to acquire information you need to advance your business and career interests. Keep in mind that the composition of your "A" team can vary according to the situation, the personalities, the geography, and the rapport your team members have with their counterparts.

Some of the most performance-driven organizations are professional sports teams: MLB, NFL, NBA, and NHL. Watch the coach of an NBA team when there is a break in the action. When a time out is called, the coach is not focusing his time and energy on the guys sitting on the bench. The coach is talking to the five guys who are in the game, those players the coach thinks can best put the team in the position to win.

It is simply good business to invest your time and energy in those areas where you can achieve your greatest return. I am not saying you should turn your back on the guys on the bench. Those may be "A" players at some point. Rethink who those individuals are who will put you in the best position to win your game—the game of achieving superior business and career success—and do it in less time and with less wasted energy. Invest your time in the 2 percent, not the 98 percent.

Do you have an "A" team? What does your "A" team look like? Who is on your "A" team? A lot of people have "B" team players. "B" team players can be your friends, they can be nice to be around, but B team players don't help you advance your career. Those people who really break through and achieve extraordinary success have "A" players on their team. Let's take a look at what I am talking about.

By the time you are thirty-five years of age with a career in the United States, you will have made contact with approximately three thousand working/career people. Think about the people you have met in your life: grade school, Little League, neighbors, high school, college, etc. You remain in communications with some of your contacts because it is in yours and the other person's best interest to do so. However, over time, your universe of contacts changes because your career and your personal goals change. The value you are able to bring to those contacts and the value they offer you is no longer the match it once was.

How many of your friends in grade school do you stay in touch with compared to the number of your college classmates? As your career advances and evolves, so must your circle of friends who make up your "A" team.

By keeping in mind your answers to a few important questions, you are continuing to fine-tune your universe of valued contacts. You continue to develop your "A" team. Here are the questions:

- Who do you spend your time with?
- What do they do with their lives?
- How ambitious are they? How successful have they been?
- How happy, optimistic, and enthusiastic are they?

Evaluate carefully if those people will really be those who will help you get to the next level you want to achieve. Do they push you forward when you come to them with new ideas, no matter what? Or do they tell you that what you have in mind won't work? Or do they just not respond? Will they advocate for you?

Make a choice of who in your list you want to continue spending time with. Don't be afraid if early on only a few people meet the standard of excellence you want to set for yourself. You should be constantly building your roster of quality people with whom you invest your time and energy. It's important to maintain contact with career friends on a regular basis—not just when you need something. Close friends do not necessarily make your "A" team, and "A" team players are not necessarily good friends. You need to identify ways you can help your career friends achieve their career and business objectives as well.

There will be an ebb and flow to this process. You will benefit by distinguishing between your golf and fishing buddies and individuals who can advance your career. Remember the eloquent words of the great golf legend and humanitarian icon, Arnold Palmer: "The road to success is always under construction."

At this point, you are producing stakeholders—individuals who can have a positive or negative impact on your career. These positive individuals are those with whom you continue to exchange high levels of value. They have an interest in what you do, and they may be affected by your work. They are important to your success

All your relationships are assets of some sort. It's helpful to remember this as you communicate with others each day. Every little act you do or fail to do adds an impression into the file that constitutes your reputation. And reputations are your currency and should be planned and managed intentionally. The more consciously and relentlessly you cultivate each relationship and bring value or joy to those you connect with, the more currency you will be amassing for future opportunities.

The *self-similarity principle* states that, when you make network contacts, you tend to choose people who resemble you in terms of experience, training, worldview, and so on—clones of yourself. Uzzi and Dunlap have found that executives disproportionately use the self-similarity principle to build their networks. Obviously, it's easier to trust someone who views the world through the same lens you do; you expect that person to act as you would in ambiguous situations. What's more, working with people who share your background is generally very efficient: You both recognize concepts that allow you to transfer information quickly and are less likely to challenge one another's ideas. Finally, like-minded people will usually affirm your point of view and, as a result, gratify your ego.

However, additional research by Uzzi and Dunlap shows that too much similarity restricts your access to discrepant information, which is crucial to both creativity and problem-solving. If all your contacts think the way you do, who will question your reasoning or push you to expand your horizon? It's easy to surround yourself with yes-men; much more difficult to surround yourself with those whose opinions always don't agree with the views you hold.

According to Noreena Hertz in the *Harvard Business Review*, "When group members are actively encouraged to openly express divergent opinions, they not only share more information, they consider it more systematically and in a more balanced and less biased way. When people engage with those with different opinions and views from their own, they become much more capable of properly interrogating critical assumptions and identifying creative alternatives."[11]

Linus Pauling, one of only two people to win a Nobel Prize in two different areas and considered one of the towering geniuses of the twentieth century, attributed his creative success not to his immense brainpower or luck but to his diverse contacts: "The best way to have a good idea is to have a lot of ideas." While expertise has become more specialized during the past fifteen years, organizational, product, and marketing issues have become more interdisciplinary, which means that individual success is tied to the ability to transcend natural skill limitations through others. Highly diverse network ties, therefore, can help you develop more complete, creative, and unbiased views of issues. And when you trade information or skills with people whose experiences differ from your own, you provide one another with unique, exceptionally valuable resources.[12]

Network theory considers close friendships to be strong ties, defined as network contacts who have a close relationship, who disclose personal, nonpublic information, and who share resources without concern for balanced and timely reciprocity. By sharing information strategically, individuals with a diverse set of connections become highly desirable information brokers, increasing their value as potential network contacts.[13]

The importance of a few close allies cannot be overstated. You alone cannot achieve your highest potential. You need a few select alliances that can help you do that. Your choice of alliances and how you build them is extremely important. With exceptionally strong alliances, you can transform your life and career and the life and careers of others for the better.

---

[11] HBR. September 12, 2013.
[12] Robert Wallace Olson. *The Art of Creative Thinking*. 1980. Page 69.
[13] Marsden & Campbell 2012.

CHAPTER 3

Highest and Best Use

For about ten years, I drove on Sunset Boulevard from our West Los Angeles residence to my office in downtown Los Angeles. At the corner of Sunset Boulevard and Highland Avenue are two landmarks: Hollywood High School and a coffee/doughnut shop. Let me correct that. There *were* two landmarks. One remains: Hollywood High School. The coffee/doughnut shop? Well, let me explain.

Every morning, when I drove by or stopped at the intersection of Sunset Boulevard and Highland Avenue, I saw the owner standing in front of his coffee shop, waving a large American flag. He wasn't tinkering with this flag. Instead, he was energetically flailing away, swinging the flag diagonally, horizontally, and every which way he could. I assume he was trying to garner attention to this business. Either that or he was having a bad acid trip!

Anyone who purchases items—and that is all of us—knows that the retail business model is changing rapidly. In spite of the proliferation of online shopping, the stand-alone, brick-and-mortar businesses understand the old adage that says the three most important factors for retail success are location, location, and location. That coffee/doughnut shop owner had a great location for his business because a lot of people traveled through that intersection. According to a survey by the Los Angeles Department of Transportation, an average of 128,000 cars pass through the intersection of Sunset Boulevard and Highland Avenue every twenty-four hours. That's the equivalent of having every man, woman, and child in Santa Monica *and* Beverly Hills travel through every day, one person per vehicle.[14]

In all my travels at that intersection, I never saw a motorist make a fast turn into that coffee-shop parking lot because he saw that flag waving in the air. The shop owner's heart was in the right direction. He was doing what he thought he should do to help make his business successful. Unfortunately, investing time and energy waving that flag was a misguided priority. Focusing on inventory, pricing, personnel, or a host of other retail-management issues could have helped keep him in business. That coffee shop is no longer there.

Each and every day we have a variety of choices how we spend our time and energy. One method for helping you determine best choices is to identify and eliminate lesser-valued activities. The late Peter Drucker, management consultant and author extraordinaire, was asked what was an important tenant that leaders should embrace to achieve exceptional business and career success. His reply was simple yet pronounced: "Find out what is not working, and stop doing it."

Low-value activities are candidates for "stop doing." Here are some low-value uses of time. Feel free to add your own low-value activities to this list:

- Activities that you are not very good at doing
- Activities other people want you to do that really do not need to be done
- Activities that have always been done this way that aren't working
- Activities that are often interrupted by people, phone calls, and other distractions
- Answering the telephone when it doesn't need to be answered
- Things you do not enjoy doing

---

[14] "Westside Has L.A.'s Busiest Intersections: Traffic: A city survey attributes the rush of cars to population growth and the area's attractions." Nancy Hill-Holtzman, *Los Angeles Times* staff writer. January 6, 1991.

YOUR SECRET WEAPON

- Failing to resolve issues with time-consuming, difficult people
- Multitasking
- Spending too much time on your e-mail
- Checking your e-mail too frequently
- Not knowing how to say no when others ask you to do things that you do not need to do

Certain research suggests that the perils of e-mails are greater than many assume. Justin Kruger, a professor at New York University's Stern School of Business, has found that as few as 50 percent of users grasp the tone or intent of an e-mail and that most people vastly overestimate their ability to relay and comprehend messages accurately.[15]

Furthermore, a study by researchers at the University of California at Irvine monitored interruptions among office workers and found that workers took an average of twenty-five minutes to recover from interruptions such as phone calls or answering e-mails and return to their original work. So trying to get more done by constantly cycling through different screens on your computer will actually hurt your productivity.[16]

I am not suggesting you eliminate e-mails. I am suggesting you think about the quality of your communications no matter what form you use. Misuse of e-mail or other forms of communications only adds to the barriers between two people trying to communicate with each other. Therefore, when logistically possible, meet face-to-face. The highest quality personal communication is face-to-face. Through continued study of communications, we can make our contact with stakeholders all the more effective.

My candidate among these ten low-value activities that need elimination as soon as possible—things you do not enjoy doing. Now I can hear you saying, "Wait a minute, Sabol. I get paid to do some things I really don't enjoy doing. There are just some things I

---

[15] Kruger, J., Epley, N., Parker, J., & Ng, Z. (2005). "Egocentrism over e-mail: Can people communicate as well as they think?" *Journal of Personality and Social Psychology.*

[16] Inc. Magazine. May 4, 2017.

have to do. It's really not my choice." If it is not your choice, then whose choice is it when it comes to decisions affecting your career?

It's your choice. Allow me to make a reference to one of the finest professors I had in graduate school, Richard R. Stephenson, PhD, University of Minnesota and former Green Beret. Dr. Stephenson exclaimed, to the bewilderment of more than one student in the class, that you are exactly where you want to be at any given time. He pointed out that if you wanted to be basking in the sun on Kaanapali beach in Maui rather than at his 8:00 a.m. human relations class, you would be on that beach.

I have thought deeply about that concept. I agree with Dr. Stephenson. You are exactly where we want to be at this very moment. We have free will. We make choices every day that affect us. I dreamed of being on that beach in Maui. Since I wanted to complete my MBA, I chose to attend his class. Maui would have to wait.

With free will comes opportunities to make intelligent choices in how we invest our time, talent, and energy. The following are high-value activities to help you achieve your business and career objectives:

Pursue those few things where you are better than others and that you enjoy the most. What are you really good at doing that others are not? Separate yourself from your competition by acquiring greater knowledge than those with whom you compete.

- *Activities you have always wanted to do.* Find activities that get you excited about your work. When your feet hit the floor in the morning, you need to be energized about how you will invest eight-plus hours of your time that day.
- *Activities that utilize your creativity.* Creativity separates one professional from another. Think about it. Whatever you do for a living, you will have competition. You can match the technical skills of your competitors. You can match their energy and their will to succeed. That is not likely to separate yourself from those with whom you compete.

  Let me give you an example of what I am talking about. My career has included heading the west coast office of a Boston-based advertising and PR firm. Depending on their location and other criteria, good copywriters in the advertising agency business are compensated around $100,000 per year. The creative director of the firm for whom I worked was paid $650,000 per annum. Why? The answer is in his title: creative director! Do I need to say anything more?

- *Activities by others that have been highly productive that you can apply to your current career.* Learn from others who have been highly successful. How did they invest their time in building their careers? What are the two or three most important skills they applied that made a difference in their success? Can you apply these skills to help you achieve your business or career interests?
- *Reduce TV Time.* The thing that Americans do most often with their free time is not cooking or exercising or hiking or any other seemingly salutary activity. No, Americans watch TV. We love to watch television. The average American watches more than five hours of live television every day according to the Nielsen media ratings company. When we look at the TV habits of wealthy people, we get a much different picture.

According to Thomas Corley, author of *Rich Habits: The Daily Success Habits of Wealthy Individuals*, approximately 67 percent of rich people watch television for one hour or less per day while only 23 percent of less-wealthy people limit their TV intake. They also generally avoid reality shows—only 6 percent of the wealthy watch them, compared to 78 percent of the non-wealthy. Rich folks simply choose more productive ways to spend their time.

Taking time away from TV to exercise, for example, can reduce the size of your waistline. Taking time away from TV to do something really challenging, like *thinking*, may just increase the size of your bank account.

Your time and how you use it are among your greatest assets. According to billionaire investor and business icon Warren Buffet, there is one thing that separates successful people from everyone else. The key, according to Buffett, is to free up more of the one thing that even billionaires can't buy. "People are going to want your time. It's the only thing you can't buy. I can buy anything I want, basically, but I can't buy time."[17]

- *Read More.* Additionally, according to Corley, 86 percent of the wealthy love to read, with an impressive 88 percent claiming that they read for self-improvement for thirty minutes or more per day. Most of them have a wealth of knowledge in all kinds of fields because they read a lot. "The rich read to acquire or maintain knowledge," he said. Corley found that they tended to read three types of books: biographies of successful people, self-help or personal development books, and history books.

While an increasing volume of the news we receive is digitally driven, we still have newspapers. Try to make reading the newspaper one of your morning habits. A newspaper can be delivered to your doorstep before you even wake up, giving you few excuses not to use it as a valuable resource in your pursuit of knowledge. Many newspaper publishers offer online subscriptions at a lower cost.

If you prefer to receive your information digitally, you should consider one of the many newspapers available to you at a click of a button. If you work for a company, many companies subscribe to the *New York Times, Wall Street Journal,* or the *Washington Post.* Take advantage of this freebie and gain knowledge while at work.

- *Surround yourself with great people.* The University of South Carolina men's basketball team achieved greatness in 2017 when they advanced to the NCAA Final Four for the first time in the school's history. After their win over Florida to advance to the Final Four, Frank Martin, South Carolina's

---

[17] https://www.businessinsider.com/personal-finance/good-habits-of-self-made-millionaires

coach, responded to a reporter's inquiry as to how his team was able to be so successful this season by acknowledging his players, his wife for her support, his coaches, South Carolina fans, and school administration. He responded by saying, "God keeps sending me great people to be around."

Do you have a cadre of great people to be around? What kind of people do you seek out? The more people you come in contact with, the higher the possibility to engage in intelligent and informative conversations where you can gain additional knowledge.

Since people enjoy informative yet casual conversations on interesting topics, we tend to retain this knowledge better. Cultivate friendships with intelligent, accomplished, educated people. When I say educated, I am not talking about limiting your contacts to people with professional titles and university degrees. I'm talking about people who have gained valuable knowledge from worldly experiences. You will find great business and career insight from these individuals. These friendships will produce stimulating conversations on a variety of topics exposing you to new ideas, perspectives, and understandings.

- *Purchase audiobooks.* Although audiobooks are no substitution for reading, they do permit the listener to gain access to a wealth of general knowledge while performing other tasks like commuting to work or exercising.

Search engines like Google, Yahoo, and Bing enable you to find answers to any question within seconds. Use these internet sites to discover current news, trends, and topics of interest.

- *Sign up for news alerts.* Several news outlets that post updated information often have a special notification system that you can subscribe to. Anytime news appears under a category that interests you, the alert will notify you on an electronic device like a cell phone, keeping you updated with current information. Some of the more-popular news-alert sites are Google and Fox News, along with BBC and AP News.

- *Register for an online class.* With today's free flow of information, you can join a full-fledged university class online with little or no cost to you. Several top universities like MIT, Harvard, and Stanford provide top-of-the line courses in everything from philosophy to politics in MOOC (massive open online course) platforms. There are currently more than ten million people taking online MOOC classes.

Taking a MOOC course will give you updated information on various specializations and the possibility of discovering new interests. MOOCs provide opportunities for you to learn alongside a group of diverse professions and professionals from every corner of the globe.

While all these activities are important, there is one activity that exceeds all others for achieving your business and career objectives: developing advocates. The next chapter begins our exploration of *how* to develop advocates. The seven-step process will systematically guide you through how to transform your contacts into advocates. Thus, transforming your career to an entirely new level of success.

CHAPTER 4

Developing Advocates

Not long ago, I came across a statement that caught my attention and perfectly summarizes a very important point: "Dying in your office is not a retirement strategy!" If you are still working, you have a chance to create your strategy and shape your legacy. The need for a positive legacy is great. People remember those who create a positive, lasting legacy. People are inspired by favorable legacies. Do you have a strategy that will get you where you want to be when your career is over? What will be your legacy?

We all have something in common with The Walt Disney Company. Those who work for Disney are not called employees; rather, they are called cast members. And these cast members do not work in an office or facility; they work "on stage." So do we.

When you take that last look at yourself standing on life's stage, what will that audience of your former employers, coworkers, employees, among others you have impacted in your life say about you? How will you be remembered? These are important questions to ask yourself because your legacy is priceless. Some day you will trade in that car you are driving. You'll shed those shoes because you need new ones. You can't shed your legacy.

In many workplaces, the more valued you are as an employee, the more positive exposure you will receive. Earning a promotion is a result—not the cause—of what and who you are. Building your legacy consists of action you take to elevate your relationship with stakeholders; to make your relationship more meaningful with those stakeholders. Legacy is about specific action you take to turn your stakeholders into one of your greatest assets: Advocates!

Let's understand what is meant by an advocate. An advocate is a person who argues for, works for, publicly supports or recommends a particular policy, cause, or person. They are individuals who devote substantial energy, time, and talent to advance the interests of others. In a nutshell, advocates want *you* to succeed and are open to helping you do just that.

Advocates are:

- Happy clients/customers
- Good friends
- People who appreciate your technical or management abilities
- People who may pay your salary or your commission
- Individuals who say nice things about you
- People who want to spend time with you and perhaps even time with your family

More importantly, we want to develop advocates beyond the basic level because advocates are much more than that. As mentioned in chapter 2, stakeholders are individuals who can have a positive impact or a negative impact on your career and your life. Advocates are stakeholders with whom you have made an emotional connection that is strong enough to proactively want to do things that support your individual professional goals.

The advocates we want:

- Go above and beyond the call of duty on your behalf
- Say great things about you when you are not around
- Open doors to decision makers who have authority and resources to help you
- Help you make more money in less time

YOUR SECRET WEAPON

- Provide you with vital information for making strategic decisions
- Always make time for you when you need it
- Pick up the phone and make a call on your behalf when asked to do so
- Tell you the truth.

As important as anything else, advocates tell you the truth when you need it most. Equally important is that you need to listen and to act on the truth that you might not want to hear. If you are not committed to taking the action recommended by that individual, then don't ask for his/her opinion.

We all have friends. At least, I hope you do. For married men who are reading this passage, please keep the following in mind: you don't want your wife having to rent pallbearers for your funeral because you don't have six friends. We all need advocates. Build your team of advocates sooner rather than later.

Having friends for life can be rewarding. Sharing similar ideals, watching them grow as you grow with them, and knowing you can talk openly with someone can all be nice experiences. These individuals represent a certain value to you, and you, likewise, represent a certain value to them. These are nice relationships to have. But there is a big difference between the value you will receive from a lifelong friend and the value you will receive from a lifelong advocate. How your lifelong advocates feel about you and what they say to others about you can influence your revenues, and your careers equal to or greater than the value provided by your lifelong friends.

Turning stakeholders into advocates requires you to provide your stakeholders with extraordinary value. Identifying methods for adding extraordinary value becomes more apparent when you understand as much as you can about each stakeholder. What is your stakeholder's business agenda, or his or her personal agenda? What does this person want to achieve in his capacity as CEO, managing director, financial director, etc.? What does she want to achieve on a personal level for her company, division, or department? Where does she want her career to take her in the next three years?

Introducing others to deal makers and other influential people or providing information unique to his or her business/industry are other examples of activities your stakeholders will value. Knowing how to help others achieve their objectives produces the kind of utility your stakeholders value. In return, they will become the advocates we want.

Keep in mind that there is distinct difference between an advocate and a friend. Let me explain. After years of working as the vice president of a Fortune 500 company, a friend of mine, was informed that he would no longer be in this role. When asked what he was planning to do now that he would soon be out of work, he replied that he was going to put his network together. Wait a minute. The moment that you become unemployed is not the right moment to begin putting your network together. That is the moment when you should be contacting your already-put-together network of advocates.

When you are unemployed, you need more than a network. You need advocates you can turn to with dialogue something like this: "Hello, John, this is Richard. I received some bad news the other day. I am no longer with XYZ company. I have a favor to ask. Will you please phone your friend, the marketing VP at ABC Company, and see if I can get an interview? I know this company well, and I strongly believe I can help them." If John makes the call, he is an advocate. If he doesn't make that call, he may be your friend. He is not an advocate. It is as simple as that.

I call this the "$10,000 Advocate Test." Can you pick up the phone and have a conversation similar to this, "Hi, Tom, this is Byron. How are you doing? Nice to hear your voice again. Listen, Tom, I need a favor. I hope you can help me out. I need $10,000. You know me. I'll pay you back as soon as I can. I'm not going to use the money for anything illegal. I wouldn't do anything like that. I really don't want to sign a note. I just need the ten grand, say, within two days"? If Byron gets the money from Tom, Byron has an advocate. If Byron doesn't get the money from Tom by Friday, Byron doesn't have an advocate; he has a friend. There is a huge difference between a friend and an advocate.

YOUR SECRET WEAPON

Do you have such a relationship with one or more people who would make certain that you received the $10,000? There is nothing magical about the figure of $10,000. The acid test for this type of relationship may be less than ten grand. However, if you don't think money is important, you have never heard of divorce!

If there is one word that describes your relationship with a person who you can count on to deliver the $10,000, that one word is trust. A friend, Steve Loranger, former president and CEO of ITT Corporation, offers this excellent definition of trust: "Trust means creating a relationship grounded on one's ability to feel comfortable that the other person is indeed a partner, working to a common goal to create a success that both parties can effect in a greater way than each could individually."

You probably have a banking relationship that includes a checking account. In this checking account, you deposit money, and you withdraw money. Think of your relationship-building as your own "personal trust bank account." This might appear to be common sense, but what is common sense is not always common behavior.

Make deposits into your "trust bank account" based on three principles: (1) say, (2) do, (3) follow through. Focus on your capability to repeat a pattern of actions that tell people "you do what you say." It is really character and competence that permeate the relationship and contribute to establishing trust. Remember: the trust you create with others has to be earned. Start making those regular deposits so you will have an account worth drawing on when you need it.

For those who are sales professionals, do not be offended by the following: your advocates are more persuasive and more credible than you are! That means they make better marketers than many sales professionals. The reason is simple. Prospective clients want to hear from their peers. They want to know about your capabilities or about your firm's capabilities from individuals they know and trust. People listen to people they like and buy from people they trust. Their trust in you is strongly influenced by what others, who have firsthand knowledge of your skills, competence, and personality, have to say about you.

The best sales pitch is delivered by individuals who have benefitted from their experience with you. Saint Mary's College at Notre

Dame Indiana understands this point when it comes to recruiting potential students. Saint Mary's provides a list of parents whose daughters have graduated from that college. I am on that list.

One evening I received a phone call from a parent in Los Angeles, asking my opinion of Saint Mary's as they were considering having their daughter attend the college. I said the following: "I have made money in various investments, and I have lost money in certain investments. The best return on any investment I have ever received was having our daughter experience four years at Saint Mary's College and graduate from that incredible institution." The parent with whom I was speaking replied, "I don't need to hear any more." Their daughter graduated from Saint Mary's College in the class of 2013.

Your stakeholders must have confidence in you before they will say great things about you; before they will "sell" for you. It's important to clearly identify who your stakeholders are and to determine what they think of you before you seek their support. All the more reason to know the answer to that all-important question: "How likely is that you would recommend me to a friend or colleague?"

When you convert customers or stakeholders into advocates, they make promoting your cause or selling your products or services so much easier. No one can be more convincing than a customer/client who is a true advocate of yours. If you can get your advocate customers to share their successes with you, they will deliver the greatest sales pitch you could ever ask for.

Remember that an advocate relationship is a very special relationship. In particular, your advocates have benefitted from you in some meaningful way. They are willing to help you when you need them. They don't just do something for you when you request it. Advocates actively seek people who will support your effort and advance your career.

If you are hesitant to make contact with a potential customer or influencer, you are not alone. The hesitation to initiate first contact with prospective customers on a consistent basis is the reason, more than any other factor, for the failure of sales professionals and other business generators to increase sales. Call Reluctance Syndrome is a condition where individuals—especially salespeople—become afraid to reach out and make phone calls.

Shannon Goodson and George Dudley, cofounders of Behavioral Sciences Research Press, point out in their book, *The Psychology of Sales Call Reluctance,* that call reluctance is the reason why 80 percent of new salespeople fail in their first year and 40 percent of sales veterans are at threat of experiencing decreasing sales.

A former Phoenix-based client of mine is a perfect example of someone suffering from call reluctance. As we discussed his employment and construction law client-generation efforts, he pointed out considerable information about one of his prospects.

He proceeded to tell me that the president of his targeted prospect company is Bill, and the general manager is Bob. They told my client that they use Acme for their tax work and corporate work, but they expected to have a need for his services in the employment area and would be sending him work when the need arose.

My client also learned that his prospect had some environmental concerns and that they were using a consultant. Their business was growing, and they expected to acquire two facilities in the Tucson area where there is a shortage of motel rooms. They were also planning to expand to other cities in the southwest.

At the end of his describing this highly valuable information he had about his prospect, he said, "No work has come in." Upon hearing this, I asked him how long it had been since he had communicated with either Bob or Bill. He replied, eighteen months!

Rather than pick up the phone and talk to his prospect, he was waiting for the phone to ring. The lawyer had considerable information that he could have used to start a conversation with Bill or Bob. When you have meaningful information to initiate dialogue with a prospect, use it to yours and your prospect's advantage. Waiting for the phone to ring is not a business-development strategy!

To overcome any hesitation to make that first contact with a prospective customer or influencer, remember you have resources to help you: your mentor and your advocate. Seek input from your mentor on how best to approach your prospect. If your mentor was in your shoes, what would be the first action step he/she would take to secure a face-to-face meeting with a prospect?

When you have established an advocate relationship, you should feel comfortable asking your advocate to make the introductory call for you. Here is another value of having a cadre of advocates you can call upon: you won't wear out any one advocate asking them to do something for you.

Before seeking your advocate's help, you need to demonstrate to him/her that you can bring value to your targeted prospect. Without a valid reason to meet with your prospect, you risk putting your advocate in an uncomfortable position when seeking his assistance. Without a valid business reason, you represent more of an imposition than a valued advisor. Valued advisors don't waste prospects' time.

A valid business reason addresses the following concerns your prospect likely has: "I am busy. Why should I spend time with you?" Or, "You really want to sell me something, right?" Wrong! If you are knowledgeable of the stakeholder's business, and you stay current with issues that affect the stakeholder's business, you will have no problem determining issues that can bring value to that prospect.

The issue often preventing the identification of a valid business reason is due to professionals not knowing enough about their prospect's organization. As an example, I was consulting to a large professional service firm in Indiana when one of that firm's partners, who had been working for a major client for quite some time, didn't know how to correctly pronounce the client company's name. Needless to say, he didn't know much about the client's business either. Had he acquired adequate knowledge of the client organization, he would be in position to craft an advocate relationship and to generate additional new business for his service firm. That never happened. Even seemingly small things, like correctly pronouncing company or personnel names, can make a difference.

To assist in recognizing a valid business reason, let's consider some information that will help you do just that. The following information should be gathered before attempting to meet with that prospect or influential person. You do not need to know answers to all these questions, but you do need to gain an understanding of how you can help the prospective client or advocate in some meaningful way. You will find, buried within answers to these questions, your valid business reason:

- What are the strategic plans for this organization?
- Is this a declining or emerging industry?
- What is the stakeholder organization's financial condition?
- What does the stakeholder's organization chart look like?
- Who are influencers in deciding to use the services you or that your firm provides?
- Who are this organization's major competitors?
- Are there any recent changes the organization has experienced?
- Does this organization have plans to expand or contract its operations?
- What is the personnel and labor environment like?
- Are they hiring or downsizing personnel?

Finding useful information on publicly held companies is relatively simple. Finding meaningful information on private companies is a bit more challenging. Here are a few resources for acquiring information on both public and private organizations:

- *American City Business Journals* (ACBJ) is the largest publisher of metropolitan business newsweeklies in the United States, with forty-three business publications across the country reaching more than four million readers each week. The business journals are available for the following cities:

Albany	Charlotte
Albuquerque	Chicago
Atlanta	Cincinnati
Austin	Columbus
Baltimore	Dallas
Birmingham	Ft. Worth
Boston Buffalo	Dayton Denver

Greensboro	Orlando
Hartford	Philadelphia
Honolulu	Phoenix
Houston	Pittsburgh
Jacksonville	Portland
Kansas City	Raleigh
Los Angeles	Sacramento
Louisville	San Antonio
Memphis	San Francisco
Milwaukee	San Jose
Miami	Seattle
Fort Lauderdale	St. Louis
Minneapolis	Tampa Bay
Saint Paul	Washington DC
Nashville	Wichita

- *The Book of Lists* provides essential information on leading buyers, businesses, and employers in over sixty of the US markets and a snapshot of local economies. (http://www.bizjournals.com/bizbooks/)

- *Corporate Yellow Book* contains highly useful information on private and public US-based companies. Information available includes names, titles, addresses, office locations, and related information. (www.leadershipdirectories.com)

- *Dun & Bradstreet*

  The company's database contains information on more than 235 million companies across two hundred countries worldwide. Often referred to as D&B, the company provides commercial data to businesses on credit history, business-to-business sales and marketing, counterparty risk exposure, supply chain management, lead scoring and social-identity matching. (http://www.dnb.com/about-us.html)

YOUR SECRET WEAPON

- *Experian* is an important source of business credit information. Records on liens, judgments, bankruptcies, UCC filings, and other items may identify potential problems and credit risk. Experian business credit reports allow you to access these types of public records as well as other key business information. (http://www.experian.com/small-business/business-public-records.jsp)

- *Financial Yellow Book* contains public and private companies that represent numerous categories of the financial industry, ranging from top accounting firms to leading brokerage firms ranked by total consolidated capital to property and casualty insurance companies and life and health-insurance companies (including holding companies) with assets over $3 billion. (www.leadershipdirectories.com)

- *PrivCo* (Private Company Financial Information) is a source for private company business and financial intelligence that covers over five hundred thousand private companies. PrivCo focuses its coverage on US major private companies (with at least $50–100 million in annual revenues), including thousands of companies that earn well under $10 million per year in annual revenue. PrivCo includes information on investment banks, private equity firms, law firms, corporate development teams, consulting firms, and major media. PrivCo also provides financial research coverage on what they consider to be smaller but high-value private companies.

- *Reference USA*—a leading provider of business and consumer research with database access to more than twenty-four million businesses. This service is available through libraries in the United States at no cost to the library member.

- *Info USA* contains same data resources as Reference USA but is not a free service.

If you have been moderately diligent in your premeeting research, you should feel comfortable asking these questions:

- *What are some of the most pressing issues your organization faces?* Note: If you have conducted premeeting research, you may already know the answer to this question. If you don't have this information, ask the question!
- *What issues are currently affecting (specific segment of) your industry?*
- *How do these issues affect your company?*
- *Can you tell me something about your strategic direction?*
- *What are the objectives for your division/department?*
- *Who might be able to give me that information?*
- *How do you see that happening?*
- *How do you feel about the recent changes?*
- *In your judgment, what is the best way?*
- *Tell me about your view of what the best solution might be for your area.*
- *What concerns or issues haven't we discussed?*
- *What should I have asked that I didn't ask?*

To develop the exceptional relationship that will turn stakeholders into your valued advocates, let's turn to the first of our seven steps.

CHAPTER 5

Attitude

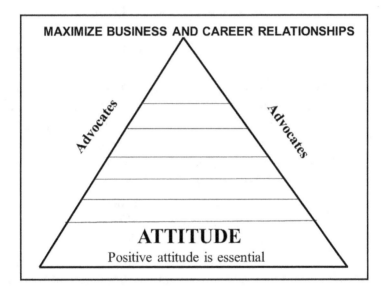

Step one in the systematic process of turning stakeholders into valued advocates is attitude. We start with attitude because it drives one's behavior. Your attitude drives the action you take. Your body language is a result of your mental attitude. You have a choice as to what attitude to adopt. If you feel angry about something that happens, that is how you choose to feel. Nothing in the event itself makes it absolutely necessary for you to feel that way. It's your choice. And since you have a choice, most of the time you are better off choosing to react in a positive rather than a negative way.

Your attitude is the first thing people pick up during face-to-face communication. When you are operating from inside a positive attitude, such as enthusiasm, curiosity, and humility, your body language sends out messages of openness.

Researchers at the University of Texas and at North Carolina State University studied 1,500 people for seven years and found that people who maintained a positive attitude were significantly less likely to show signs of aging; they were less likely to become frail and were more likely to be stronger and healthier than those that had a negative attitude. These researchers found that positive thinking and a positive attitude improved a person's health because it made it more likely that they would succeed in life. Not only will a positive attitude help you be healthy and live longer; it will also increase the likelihood that you will succeed.[18]

Our attitude is also a sales tool. You can be a brilliant technician, lawyer, secretary, plumber, teacher, but remember: people buy all of you. They buy your competencies, your personality, your appearance, your command of language, and most importantly, they buy your attitude. Some people embrace a positive attitude, and some don't. Those who understand the value of a positive attitude have opportunities to create favorable experiences with their stakeholders. A lot of people miss those opportunities because they fail to grasp the first of our seven steps: attitude. Allow me to make the following analogy.

My wife and I planned to purchase a ten-acre residence west of Orlando, Florida. I contacted a real estate partner in central Florida's largest law firm. My communication with that lawyer was limited to phone, e-mail, and fax. In the contract to purchase this property, I had the lawyer include several contingencies, which I later exercised. We chose not to purchase the property.

It has been over fifteen years since that transaction, and I have never heard from that lawyer. A phone call saying something like, *Hi, Byron are you still alive?* Better yet: *Whatever happened to that property you were interested in purchasing?* Don't knock yourself out.

---

[18] Trisha and John Parker. "The Best of Our Lives: Sharing the Secrets of a Healthy and Happy Retired Life." Chapter 2.

YOUR SECRET WEAPON

How about a phone call—say, ever five years or so—asking me how I am doing?

Is a two-minute phone call too much to ask? I wouldn't know this individual if he walked into my office. And that is not the only time I have had that kind of experience. Here's my point: I have had opportunities to refer people to a variety of professionals. My wife, an executive with an international corporation, had opportunities to refer people to numerous professionals. Not only will that lawyer never get a referral from us; that law firm will never get a referral from me. As far as I am concerned, he is the face of my experience with that firm.

Now some people may think that is a very narrow perspective to have on the entire firm. You know what? That may be true. I may be a bit narrow in my judgment of the entire firm. I was also the client not just of that lawyer; I was a client of that law firm. I am the consumer, and in today's competitive business environment, consumers rule. They have more choices for services and products. They have more buying power than ever. Consumers today make the call on who they hire, what they say about who they hire, and to whom they refer potential new business.

Let me give you another example of what I am talking about when I say some people let their misguided attitude interfere with their career, their revenue-generation potential, and the capacity to assist others. One of the services I have provided clients based outside the United States is identifying individuals within the United States who may represent a possible business nexus for both parties through face-to-face meetings.

For one of my European-based clients, I contacted partners of several large law firms in Seattle and in San Francisco who enthusiastically agreed to meet with my client. However, when I phoned a partner in the Century City office of a Los Angeles-based firm, I got a much different response.

I introduced myself and was about to end my describing the purpose of my call when the person on the other end of the phone abruptly shouted, "I don't take those kinds of meetings." *Bang!* Down went his phone. Upon hearing his response, my immediate thought was, *Bad attitude!*

If I was to offer a defense for his behavior, I might think, "Well, he is really busy, and he just doesn't have the time to discuss a possible new business relationship that may benefit him and his law firm." However, I am not offering a defense for his response for a very simple reason. Within the service firm profession, there is a concept known as *proliferation.* Simply put, proliferation means that if a fee earner is too busy to take on new work or too busy to meet to discuss a potential new business relationship, then that fee earner passes the potential new work opportunity to a fellow partner or to a younger fee earner who needs the work opportunity and is, of course, qualified to do the work.

Not to be discouraged, I found a much different response when I phoned that firm's downtown Los Angeles office. I called the same department as that of the partner in their Century City office who so energetically hung up his phone on me. I was halfway through my remarks with the downtown partner when he said, "When can your client be here?" These two professionals had identical titles, worked in the same department for the same firm, but what a contrast in attitude.

> *Just like a great building stands on a strong foundation, so does success. And the foundation of success is attitude.*
> —William James (1842–1910)
> Harvard University Psychologist and Philosopher)

Charles R. Swindoll is the founder of *Insight for Living*, which airs a radio program of the same name on more than two thousand stations around the world in fifteen languages. He pinpoints the value of attitude by exclaiming, "The longer I live, the more I realize the impact of attitude on my life. Attitude to me is more important than education, than circumstances, than money, than failures, than success, than what other people think, say, or do. It's more important than appearance, giftedness, or skill. The remarkable thing is, we have a choice every day regarding the attitude we will embrace for that day."[19]

---

[19]   Charles Swindoll. "Grace Awakening." Thomas Nelson Inc; Workbook Edition.

YOUR SECRET WEAPON

In a world where we cannot control every circumstance or every person, we do have control over ourselves. Swindoll understands how to do that. He points out, "We cannot change our past. We cannot change the fact that people will act in a certain way. We cannot change the inevitable. The only thing we can do is play on the one thing we can control, and that is our attitude. I am convinced that life is 10 percent what happens to me and 90 percent how I react to it. And so it is with you. We are in charge of our attitudes."[20]

A positive attitude may not solve all of your problems, but it will annoy enough people to make it worth the effort.
—Herm Albright (1876–1944)

Attitude has an immeasurable impact on organizational success. Customer acquisition is the initial step, not the ultimate goal. Great organizations have systems in place to retain their clients. You don't want your clients going down the street for services you have been providing them for years. The fact that a customer has been with you for many years is no guarantee they will continue to utilize your services.

Having the wrong attitude can do harm to relationships, even long-standing relationships. Several years ago, I was conducting a face-to-face client-satisfaction survey on behalf of my client, one of the United Kingdom's largest law firms. The person I was interviewing was a principal with the Bank of England. Included in the subject matter of this survey was *attitude*. My reference to the importance of attitude instantly incited an energetic response from the interviewee. He proceeded to tell me that the Bank of England had a long-standing relationship with one of London's premier law firms.

He also informed me that he was retiring and was ending the relationship with that law firm. How long did that firm represent the Bank of England for that specific type of work? Are you ready for this? 126 years! When I asked why he was severing this long-standing relationship, he replied, "Because their attitude is, 'We'll get there

---

[20] Charles Swindoll. "Attitude." (http://faculty.kutztown.edu/friehauf/attitude.html).

when we get there.' I've had it with their attitude." Even a century-old relationship can be cancelled because of a bad attitude. Don't take relationships for granted.

Remember Marian Kennedy, cofounder of the Kennedy Van der Laan law firm, from chapter 1? When I asked her about the importance of a favorable attitude, she responded poignantly, "I believe attitude is vital to success. Firmly knowing what success means for you in your business or in an individual project and focusing on achieving that success are important steps, but believing with all your heart that you will achieve that success is the magic ingredient. Remain critical about the actions you take and whether they truly serve your goals, as well as whether they remain true to your moral beliefs—but never question the inevitability of your success."

Let me tell you about two extraordinary people who did not fail to grasp the importance of attitude. While both individuals have passed away, their insights remain vital today. Attitude helped one of these individuals make millions of dollars for himself and for many of his employees in the insurance business. For the other person, attitude helped save a life—his own—in a Nazi concentration camp.

W. Clement Stone was a businessman, philanthropist, and book author. He was born in Chicago, Illinois, on May 4, 1902. His father died in 1905, leaving his family in debt. In 1908 he hawked newspapers on the south side of Chicago while his mother worked as a dressmaker. By 1915 he owned his own newsstand. Stone dropped out of high school to sell insurance full-time. He later received a diploma from the Young Men's Christian Association Central High School in Chicago. He later took courses at Detroit College of Law and Northwestern University.

In 1919 Stone built the Combined Insurance Company of America (a company providing accident and health-insurance coverage), and by 1930 he had over a thousand agents selling insurance for him across the United States. By 1979 Stone's insurance company exceeded $1 billion in assets. Combined Insurance Company later merged with the Ryan Insurance Group to form Aon Corporation in 1987. The Combined Insurance Company later spun off by Aon to ACE Limited in April 2008 for $2.56 billion.

YOUR SECRET WEAPON

Stone explained the importance of a positive mental attitude in his last interview not long before dying. Stone said, "A positive mental attitude is necessary for achieving worthwhile success. We in America know what it is for us, for we have inherited the tenets of the Judeo-Christian faiths on which our constitution, laws, and customs have been based. Strive to understand and apply the golden rule. Believe that any goal that doesn't violate the laws of God or the rights of your fellow men can be achieved."

Stone's understanding of the value of attitude is, perhaps, best summed up in his remarks, "There is little difference in people. That little difference is a big difference. The little difference is attitude. The big difference is whether that attitude is positive of negative. Our attitude drives our behavior. Our attitude either stimulates or stifles our enthusiasm."

And he is so right. Our attitude either stimulates us or it is a roadblock to taking the action we need to take to achieve our goals and to make things better for ourselves and for those around us.

The second person who understood the importance of attitude is Viktor Emil Frankl. Born in 1905 into a Jewish family of civil servants in Vienna, Austria, Frankl became a neurologist and psychiatrist. He also became a Holocaust survivor.

He lived with his bride, mother, father, brother, and sister in Vienna. All members of his family were thrown into concentration camps. After years in the concentration camps, including Auschwitz and Dachau, only Frankl and his sister survived. The other family members perished.

Later in life, Frankl published many books with an underlying theme of the importance of attitude. In his writings he mentions that when he was imprisoned, he frequently saw a man holding a cigarette whose hands would be trembling. Frankl knew that was the last cigarette that man would smoke. Frankl talks about how he used his attitude to help him survive those unbearable conditions. He would use his attitude when standing in front of the concertina wire that encased these poor souls, and he would think about what life would be like when he got out of prison.

Among other things, he said, "We who lived in concentration camps can remember the men who walked through the huts, comforting others, giving away their last piece of bread. They may have been few in number, but they offer sufficient proof that everything can be taken from a man but one thing: the last of the human freedoms—to choose one's attitude in any given set of circumstances, to choose one's own way."[21]

Let me emphasize that last part: "The last of the human freedoms to choose one's attitude in any given set of circumstances…to choose one's own way." What a powerful statement about a choice we all have. And guess what? The attitude you want is your choice. It's free; no cost for your attitude. No appointment is needed. You don't have to stand in line to get one. And there are no taxes to pay for your attitude. Your attitude is your decision.

If a positive attitude can help a person survive those ungodly circumstances being encased in a concentration camp, what do you think such a powerful attitude can do for you? A positive attitude is a powerful resource. Use it to yours and your stakeholders' advantage.

We can talk about a positive attitude. We can think about a positive attitude. Would it not be better for all concerned if we demonstrate that positive attitude? Here are four surefire means to demonstrate that important attitude.

Interest. Demonstrate a sincere interest in the individual rather than what he/she represents. Get to know the person before discussing business aspects. Demonstrating interest in the other person means investing time with him or her in as personal manner agreeable to the both of you. This may be in person, if geographically feasible. If you can't meet face-to-face, pick up the phone and do something really novel in this digital-driven world of ours: talk to each other.

Does your cell phone come with ears? Among your interest-demonstrating objectives is to listen to the other person. That's rather difficult when you are buried facedown on your cellphone keypad. Unless the other person demands that you only text him or her, avoid texting.

---

[21] Viktor E. Frankl. "Man's Search for Meaning." Beacon Press, Boston.

YOUR SECRET WEAPON

The more time that you are willing to spend with the person, the greater will be his tendency to trust you and to feel that you are acting in his best interest. The more obvious it is that you care about the person, about what he really needs, the more likely it is that he will be open to your influence. This is even more important in your personal relationships, with your family and friends. The more that people feel you care about them, the more open they will be to your influence.

One of your goals is to make the people talking to you feel comfortable. You achieve this comfort level by demonstrating through active listening that you are interested in what the other person has to say. You convey these important attitudes and ideas when you communicate the following to the other person:

"I am interested in you as a person."

"I think that what you believe is important."

"I respect your point of view, and even if I don't agree with it, I know it is valid to you."

"I am not trying to change or evaluate you as a person."

"I think you are worth listening to, and I want you to know that I'm the kind of person with whom you can talk."

While it is difficult to convince someone that you respect him or her by telling them so, you are much more likely to project this feeling by demonstrating respect. Listening does this most effectively. Remember: a good listener is not only popular but after a while he learns something!

There is a correlation between a vital listening experience of mine and the assassination of Martin Luther King. Let me explain. While going through basic training in the Army at Fort Polk, Louisiana, I was in charge of platoon of forty-six trainee soldiers—about a third of whom were African American, a third were Caucasian, and a third I'm not sure what they were. The day Dr. King was assassinated—April 4, 1968—was also our last day of basic training. This meant that all of us were to be assigned that day to our next gig, or as the military preferred to call it, military occupation specialty (MOS).

67

Many of the soldiers in my platoon enlisted for three years—as opposed to being drafted for two years—with the understanding that they would likely be given their MOS of choice. This was taking place during the height of the Vietnam War. Many of those men who enlisted, thinking they would be assigned the MOS they were told they would get, were assigned to Tiger Land, the infantry training center, which meant they were most likely being sent to serve in Vietnam.

Coupling the emotional impact of the assassination of Dr. King with not receiving the assignment they expected after enlisting for three years, some of the troops turned our barracks that night into a near riot. One trainee was hit in the back with a pipe, and relations between races were about to explode. What should have never been a racial issue was now a full-blown racial issue.

The solution, I believed at the time, was to figure a way to release some of the pressure that was boiling over. I called for a meeting with the leaders of the uprising and quickly found myself to be one of only two non-African Americans in a room with a dozen or so very unhappy soldiers. As we began the meeting, I listened. They yelled. I listened. They ranted. I listened some more. The more I kept quiet and focused on *how* they expressed their anger and pain, the more effective our communications became and the more their emotions subsided. We all left the next day for our MOS assignments. It didn't take a rocket scientist to understand *why* they were mad. What it did take was an opportunity for them to have someone listen to them.

Everyone wants to feel important enough to be heard. When you are having a face-to-face conversation with someone, your listening skills are being tested. Use effective listening skills to make the other person feel as though he or she is the most important person to you at that moment.

Effective listening becomes important to us when we realize it is the first step in transforming the other person into a collaborative colleague. Active, empathetic, and responsive listening takes place when we genuinely care about what the other person is trying to tell us and actively reach out with questions, tone, voice, and body language.

We improve our ability to communicate by shedding the impulse to talk and focus on what the other person has to say and how he or she says it. And that is not always easy to do, especially if you are knowledgeable about the subject at hand. There is a natural tendency, almost an urgency, for some people to interject their comment sooner rather than later.

Keep in mind that your nonverbal communications—expressions, manner, body language, tone of voice, the attitude you express—often reveal your true feelings about others and can slowly corrode critical relationships. Understanding why we don't listen is a step in the right direction for improving our listening abilities. Here are a few of the reasons we fail to listen as well as we should.

- *We are not trained to listen.* Listening is not a part of our educational system. A private high school in Orlando, Florida, offers a marine biology course that provides students with an opportunity to swim right next to manatees, which is the only reason our daughter took the course. What about a course on listening? Not to be found. I contacted the National Education Association to determine if there was a high school in the United States that offered a course, seminar of any program on listening skills. They couldn't find one.
- *My mind is elsewhere.* While we speak at the rate of 125 to 150 words per minute, we can comprehend approximately 500 words per minute. This variance creates a comprehension thought gap. The body is present while the mind is elsewhere. This gives us the opportunity to think about a lot of things other than what the other person intends.
- *I am in control when I am talking.* If you happen to be an expert on the subject of discussion, you know that there is a natural tendency for many people to take the lead and to talk about that which they know well. If we are good at what we do, we like to talk about it. If we think we know more about the subject of discussion, we like to talk about it. If we have a strong opinion on a subject—especially if

the subject strikes an emotional cord with us—we talk. It's quite difficult to listen when we talk.

- *I am thinking ahead.* By anticipating what we will say next, we risk not receiving the message the other person intended. We may be so intent on responding to the other person our focus is not on what he is saying. Our focus is on the message we are mentally crafting. When we fail to receive the other person's message, we send our own message back that what he has to say is not important.
- *I'm comfortable when I talk.* Hey, if people will listen, others will talk, particularly about themselves and their careers. Look at people on their cell phones. What are they doing? They're talking.

Here are a few tips on how to make your listening a great communications resource:

1. *Prepare to listen.* The first step in communicating is not listening. The important first step to effective listening is *preparing* to listen, which means to become physically alert and to think of the value you will receive from the information that is about to be presented. Whether you may agree with or disagree with what you hear, the point is this: there is something of value for you to listen to in the information to be presented. Otherwise, why are you there?
2. *Maintain eye contact.* Practicing good eye contact is an essential skill for effective communication. Maintaining eye contact with someone you are talking to displays interest and lets them know, "You are important, and I am actively listening."
3. *Demonstrate your understanding.* Provide meaningful feedback to the other person by occasionally restating the main points or by asking a question that proves you understand the main idea. If you don't understand the other person's idea, that's all the more reason to ask questions. The important point is not to repeat what they've said to prove you were listening but to prove you understand.

YOUR SECRET WEAPON

4. *Eliminate emotions.* Our listening abilities are impacted by our emotions. If we hear something that opposes our most deeply held ideas, concepts, or convictions, we send up a barrier as we prepare a response to what we are hearing. We turn off our reception at the risk of missing vital information. Hold off making judgments. After the person has finished presenting his or her thoughts, review the main ideas presented and then assess them.

5. *Take notes.* I distinctly recall asking two partners at a prestigious law firm in the United Kingdom if they took notes when they met with clients or with prospects. One lawyer responded that he always takes notes because he said he doesn't have a perfect memory, and he doesn't want to risk missing important information. Contrasting that response was the other lawyer who said he does not take notes because he does not want others to think that he doesn't have a great memory. Their response reminds me of the old adage: "We all have photographic memories. It's just that some of us don't have any film."

How many times have you gone to a meeting thinking that you will remember the important things, only to find yourself asking a colleague for information about issues discussed during that session? Here is my recommendation. Unless you have a photographic memory with a lot of film, put your ego aside and take notes.

How good are you at listening? This quiz enables you to quickly compare your own listening behaviors with behaviors normally thought to be associated with exceptionally good listening skills. Indicate your response using the following scale:

4 = Always   3 = Most of the time   2 = Some of the time   1 = Rarely

1. I remind myself that listening is an opportunity to learn something.
2. I make myself listen even when the subject fails to interest me.

3. I make myself listen even if I think that the speaker is not particularly bright.
4. I focus on the speaker's ideas and not on his appearance or mannerisms.
5. I try to understand the speaker's feelings as well as his/her words.
6. I wait for the speaker to finish before I form an opinion.
7. I make sure I understand the speaker's point of view before responding.
8. I show that I am engaged by maintaining eye contact, nodding, and leaning forward.
9. I am relaxed, calm, and patient when listening.
10. I do not interrupt the speaker.
11. I take notes if I must remember points being made.
12. I capitalize on lag time by reviewing in my mind the speaker's main ideas.
13. I ask nonthreatening questions to ensure that I understand.
14. I often paraphrase what I hear to be sure I have heard it correctly.
15. I do not allow distractions to divert my attention.

How do you rate?

50–60 Excellent! You have exceptional listening skills.
40–49 Above average, but you could improve your skills.
30–39 Your score is promising, but you could greatly improve.
15–29 You need serious listening training.
Less than fifteen means: You need help!

Remember: focused listening builds trust with the other person. These techniques will assist you to become a more-committed listener, encouraging others to listen when it is your time to speak:

- *Empathize.* Put yourself in the other person's shoes to better understand his/her perceptions and feelings. If you had a

YOUR SECRET WEAPON

similar experience to that of the other person, call upon that experience. Use these comments:

"I think I understand why you might feel so strongly because I had a similar experience in my life."

"I can appreciate why you feel that way."

"I understand."

Do not say: *"I know exactly how you feel."* The reason is, you can't know!

- *Acknowledge.* Encourage greater openness by recognizing and acknowledging the feelings being expressed by the other person with comments like:

  "I can see you are pretty upset about that. Can you tell me why?"

  "I can appreciate now why you feel that way."

- *Encourage comments.* Encouraging comments invites the other person to share his/her feelings, perceptions, and attitudes. Use comments like:

  "Please tell me more."

  "I'm interested in what you are saying/thinking/feeling."

  "I hear what you are saying."

  "Tell me more about why you disagree with me."

- *Ask questions.* Ask questions to solicit advice and identify possible solutions, such as:

  "How might we resolve this?"

  "What do you think we should do next?"

  "Tell me more about what you want."

  "What would you like to see happen?"

  "Why do you think that would work?"

- *Recognize contribution.* Thank the person for communicating with you. You may want to use the following:

  "I appreciate your willingness to raise these issues with me."

  "I learned a great deal from what you said, specifically…"

> "*I appreciate your willingness to talk to me about this.*"
> "*I didn't know you felt that way before.*"

- *Humility.* Being a little humbler allows you to focus your self-interest less and focus your attention more on the other person.

> *Humility may not be fashionable in the business world, but I am convinced that humility in companies would improve balance sheets.*
> —The Late Rev. Fr. George O'Brien (my dear friend)
> Professor at Mt. Saint Mary's College, Brentwood, California

Listening is part, although a very important part, of effective communications. There is a huge difference between knowing something—having command of product or service offerings—and passing that knowledge on to others. Clarity of communication is vital for business and career success. Communication is not about transmission. Communication is about reception! Unless the other person understands what you are saying in the same way you understand what you said, communication has failed. Through our continued study of communications, we can make our contacts with stakeholders all the more effective.

While on the dais at an event in Los Angles, I was seated next to a professor from the University of Southern California School of Business. I turned to the professor and asked him how Judy was doing. I knew Judy had been working on her DBA degree from my days with her in the Marketing Research Department at the Southern California Edison Company. The professor startled me when he replied, "She will never get her doctorate from this university." I asked why. He responded, "Because she can't communicate what is in her head!"

I thought about his comments. In a way, I tended to agree with him because there were numerous occasions when my conversations with Judy left me puzzled as to what she was trying to say. I found Judy to be highly intellectual; however, many of us—including the USC professor—found her void of needed communications skills.

YOUR SECRET WEAPON

Knowing how to effectively communicate face-to-face is vital to one's career success, such as knowing what you want to say and why. In addition, it's vital to clearly understand the purpose and intent of your message. Another concept for effective communication that does not garner as much attention, but is just as important, is the reality that words, images, and sounds mean different things to different people. An experience I had while watching the movie, *Saving Private Ryan,* brought home the importance of that concept.

I saw the film at the Odeon theatre in Leeds, England, one Saturday night. An American epic war drama set during the invasion of Normandy in World War II, the film won five Academy Awards. Early in the film an elderly World War II veteran and his family visit the Normandy American Cemetery and Memorial in Normandy, France. The veteran walks around the cemetery and, upon seeing one specific gravestone, collapses to his knees, overwhelmed by emotion.

The film flashes back to the morning of June 6, 1944, the beginning of the Normandy Invasion, as American soldiers prepare to land on Omaha Beach. They suffer heavily from their struggle against German infantry, machine-gun nests, and artillery fire. As the film graphically shows American soldiers maimed and dying, I heard laughter coming from behind me in the theater. As I looked around, I noticed several kids—maybe eight to ten years of age—giggling and laughing at what they were seeing on the screen. I also noticed older people, those with gray hair or maybe no hair, sitting transfixed on what they were seeing and hearing as the scenes played out across the screen.

We all heard the same words spoken by the soldiers, saw the same images, and heard the same sounds from that movie. What was not the same was the reaction to those words, images, and sounds. What these kids most likely failed to realize is that seventy-seven people were killed, and hundreds were injured in bombings in Leeds during that war. Unless these kids had a parent, grandparent, or teacher explain to them the severity of the bombings in Leeds, the action on the screen was pure amusement for them.

I have been present when Leeds has conducted a reenactment of the bombing of their city. Thousands of people showed up in Leeds

City Centre one Saturday night in December. That part of the city went completely dark as all lights were turned off except for huge search lights that illuminated the sky. That was followed by thunderous sounds of bombs being dropped, all intended to ensure that Leeds residents and visitors realize the pain of WWII on that country and on that city.

Words, images, and sounds mean different things to different people. The more we know about the other person's background—age, education, economics, race, religion, political persuasion, and family background—the more effectively we can anticipate that person's response to communications. The more we know about the other person, including his or her communications style, the more effective we will be in our communications with this person.

Another important ingredient for improving our ability to communicate with others is understanding something about their communications style. Understanding communications style is a priceless asset. Understanding an individual's personality and communications style allows a person to more effectively communicate and to persuade others to his or her point of view. Different personality types prefer to be persuaded and communicated in different ways. Knowledge of personality types helps us to communicate and to establish rapport with others. This also assists us to identify how people with whom you communicate like to be communicated. Through your knowledge of communication styles, you are also in a position to defuse many communication and personality conflicts.

Researchers, articulating the importance of personality and its influence on how people communicate and relate to each other, stress that each of us falls into one of four major behavioral functions: controller, analyzer, supporter, or promoter. Individuals tend to get along better with those whose communication style is similar to their own. Conversely, we have the most difficult time communicating and relating with someone who is in the exact opposite quadrant as ours. If you know your own communication style and the style of the other person, you are much better equipped to communicate in a manner that seems more open and trustworthy to the other person. As communication barriers start to fall, your ability to relate is enhanced because you are more in sync with each other.

The study of the four personality types is not an attempt to pigeonhole anyone into a specific quadrant but rather to provide information that will assist a person to align his or her communication with the communication style of the other person. The goal, then, is to assist us to be on the same wavelength as the other person. The following will help you recognize each of these communication styles and assist you to present your message so that it will be acceptable to the other person.

Controller. The *controller* is a doer and often the driving force within an organization. This person leads others. He is characterized by emphasis on action and results. This person thrives on getting things done here and now. Just as the alpha dog must lead the pack, the controller must be first and must lead. Because he places high standards on himself and others, he is likely to be seen as constructively impatient and a tireless worker.

When communicating or when working with the typical *controller,* be prepared to move fast and to be challenged. Expect the *controller* to argue, interrupt, disagree, raise her voice, and challenge your thoughts. Keep in mind that this behavior is not an attack on you. The controller's communication style is not personal; it is just the way he or she is.

Analyzer. He is characterized by analysis, details, logic, and systematic inquiry, and being a bit stiff. This person functions in a steady, tenacious manner, finding great satisfaction in identifying a problem, weighing options carefully, and testing them to determine the best possible solution. The analyzer is of great value as a logical thinker who provides objectivity to a complex problem. Don't expect him to be the life of the party, but he will show up on time!

When communicating with or when working with *analyzers,* be well organized, have details lined up, and plan each meeting carefully. Speak slowly as she processes information more carefully than most. Pause as you speak and ask questions to make sure you are both on the same page of your topic of discussion. One of the surest means for creating a communication barrier with the analyzer is to generalize. Remember: think specifics when communicating with the analyzer.

Supporter. A concern for people dominates the thinking and behavior of the *supporter* style. He is often sought out for his ability to empathize and for his patience with others during a time of crisis. An understanding listener, he can identify change in ways that reduce conflicting forces and increase the likelihood of cooperation and teamwork. A weakness among supporters is their tendency to become emotional, which may be viewed as a substitution for taking action. Of the four personality types, the supporter is the most likely to flinch—to back away—in a time of conflict.

Effective communication with the *supporter* is best achieved through an informal, open, and personalized approach. Your face-to-face communications should be somewhat guarded. Maintain ample physical space between yourself and the *supporter* type. While you can be enthusiastic, even somewhat aggressive when communicating with the *controller*, the *supporter* will balk at signs of aggressive communications.

Promoter. The big-picture person has just arrived. The *promoter* style is characterized by heavy emphasis on ideas, innovation, concepts, and long-range thinking. The promoter will challenge you not because she is hostile but because she has learned the value of constant probing to uncover new ideas.

A fast and deep thinker, she questions herself and others. She is not inclined to take things for granted. The promoter is seen as a leader and a visionary capable of seeing new possibilities that others do not sense. This is a person with a strong ego who can come across as "superior" and can be condescending in her communications. Quick thinking and a quick wit are characteristics of the promoter.

When communicating with the promoter, probe for her ideas and concepts. Ask questions of this person. Because so much of this individual's ego is invested in what she does and how she does it, communicate your awareness of her ideas, plans, and most of all, her vision. Promoters love to talk about their plans. Let them have at it. Sit back and absorb.

YOUR SECRET WEAPON

Word Choices That Stimulate Positive Responses

Each communication style responds differently to different words. Here are a few words that normally stimulate positive responses. Use these words to enhance your communications:

Controller

Planned	*Objective*
Completed	*Return on investment*
Mission	*Competitive advantage*

Analyzer

Experience	*Proven*
Factual	*Principles*

Supporter

Consensus	*Reliable*
Flexible	*Dependable*
Adaptable	*Precedent*

Promoter

Possible
Doable
Hunches
Innovative
Ingenious

The following chart provides a quick review of characteristics of the four communications styles.

Communications Style Matrix

Characteristics	Controller	Analyzer	Supporter	Promoter
Work-space:	Busy, formal, efficient, structured	Organized, functional, formal	Personal, relaxed, informal	Stimulating, personal, cluttered
Appearance:	Businesslike, functional	Formal, conservative	Casual, conforming	Fashionable, stylish
Behavioral focus:	Doing, competing, getting results	Structure, logic, organization, problem-solving	Expression, human interaction, projecting feelings	Imagination, theory, envisioning speculation
Value orientation:	Action, winning, wealth	Quality, being right, ethics	Family, friendship, loyalty	Concepts, ideology, discovery
Motivated by:	Stimulating action, achievement, controlling, gaining an edge	Logical, scientific challenge, systematic inquiry	Love, sense of contribution, recognition	Pioneering spirit, inventing, creating
Needs to know benefits:	What it does, by when, what it costs	How to justify the purchase logically, how it works	How it will affect his or her personal circumstances	How it will enhance his or her status, who else does it
Behavioral discomfort zones:	Free-form, vague, hypothetical, theoretical, moving slowly, no goal, no bottom-line	Interpersonal communications, situations requiring fast decisions	Structured situations, taking orders, impersonal, scientific, demanding accuracy	Bureaucracy, adjusting to mass psychology, making things happen quickly

YOUR SECRET WEAPON

Hobby orientation:	Competitive sports wheeling-dealing, acquiring, gambling, action games	Nonfiction books, computers, photography, collecting	Social, entertaining, family interaction, fiction, volunteering, beach scene	Reading, walking, backpacking, mountain-climbing, chess, other intellectually-oriented games
Oral communication:	Assertive, controlling, confronting	Structured, careful	Personalized, marked voice inflection	Professional, stream of consciousness, associative
Written communication:	Short, simple, directed to action	Planned, organized, geometric	Unplanned, spontaneous, warm	Technically oriented, abstract, idea-oriented
Likes you to be:	To the point	Precise	Pleasant	Stimulating
Dress preference:	Functional	Conservative	Informal	Unpredictable
Work environment preference:	Demanding, fast-paced, competitive	Ordered, neat, data at hand	Homey, comfortable	Think tank, high-tech
Wants to be:	In charge	Correct	Liked	Admired
Irritated by:	Inefficiency, indecision	Surprises, unpredictability	Insensitivity, impatience	Inflexibility, routine

CHAPTER 6

Knowledge

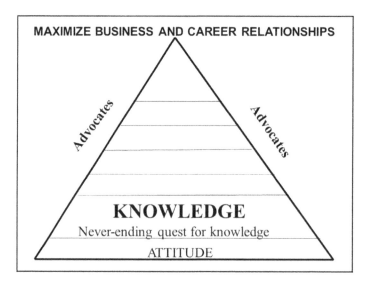

The second of our seven steps for developing advocates is found in our knowledge. Your targeted advocate must see you as an expert, not just see you as someone who is good at what you do. Being *really* good at what you do is not only at the heart of a successful career; it is crucial for getting ahead in life.

Maintaining your status as someone who is viewed as being really good at what you do requires more than expanding your technical or professional skills. You need to have a never-ending quest for knowledge. Expanding your knowledge through courses, conferences, webcasts, lectures, the Internet, and the many other resources available today is a start to maintain needed knowledge.

However, do not limit your knowledge growth to courses and sessions that qualify for continued education credit. While continued education credit can be important to maintain your technical skills level, gaining new knowledge that will arm you with value you can bring to those who are important to your career and your business success requires much more than CE credits.

Another word of caution: avoid relying solely on conference presenters, session leaders, or training resources that are limited to being members of your profession.

A never-ending quest for knowledge means to go beyond what you are comfortable doing. When the late business-management expert Peter Drucker was asked what corporate leaders need to do to stay at the top of their management responsibilities, he replied, "Learn to play the violin." Mr. Drucker was not suggesting that you pick up a Stradivarius and master the instrument. He was stressing that to remain fresh and creative in your business life, you need to do something different. You need to stretch. You need to step outside of your comfort zone and be more creative.

In his book, *Where Have All the Leaders Gone?*, the late legendary auto executive Lee Iacocca, presented his "nine Cs of leadership." The first word listed does not refer to a brilliant IQ nor is it an MBA from an Ivy League university; rather, his first C of Leadership is *curiosity*. He points out that a leader has to show curiosity. He has to listen to people outside of the "Yes, sir" crowd in his inner circle. "If a leader never steps outside his comfort zone to hear different ideas, he grows stale," Iacocca stressed. "If he doesn't put his beliefs to the test, how does he know he's right? The inability to listen is a form of arrogance. It means you think you already know it all, or you just don't care." A good leader recognizes that they might not know everything about everything, but they're curious to find the answers.[22]

When all you have that differentiates you is price, you are a commodity. But we don't want to be viewed as just a commodity. We

---

[22] Lee Iacocca. "Where Have All the Leaders Gone?" Scribner. Page 6.

must have a relationship with stakeholders that, to some degree, overrides price. If you believe you can separate yourself from competitors based on existing knowledge, think again. Knowledge itself is becoming a commodity. Knowledge dissipates quickly when people leave to work for competitors and take valuable knowledge with them.

You differentiate yourself by becoming the unique expert that others look to. You become that expert by combining high levels of curiosity and creativity. Without curiosity and creativity, you are limited to existing knowledge. There is nothing wrong with tapping into existing knowledge. We rely on a body of existing knowledge every day, but it's difficult to separate yourself from competitors when you and your competition possess the same basic product and service knowledge.

When we are curious, we are armed with the tools to view tough situations more creatively. Studies have found that curiosity is associated with less defensive reactions to stress and less aggressive reactions to provocation. We also perform better when we're curious. In a study of 120 employees, Francesca Gino, behavioral scientist and the Tandon Family Professor of Business Administration at Harvard Business School, found that natural curiosity was associated with better job performance, as evaluated by their direct bosses. Furthermore, Gino's research confirms that encouraging people to be curious generates workplace improvements.[23]

I have relatives, whom I love, who have much in common with each other: they were born in this country; they have lived their entire lives in this country, served in our country's military; they are in good health and are financially stable. They also have something else in common: they have never been to our nation's capital. They have never stood in front of the Lincoln Monument or the Vietnam War memorial and observed the fifty-eight thousand names on that wall. They have not visited the Martin Luther King Memorial and reflected on the quotations that surround Dr. King's statute.

I used to think to myself, *How can anyone who has lived in this country for any reasonable length of time not visit our nation's capital?* I

---

[23] "Why Curiosity Matters." Francesca Gino. Harvard Business Review. September–October 2018 Issue.

YOUR SECRET WEAPON

used to think that there had to be some logical explanation for this behavior. For years this was mind-boggling to me. Oh, I would ask them why, and the response was some lame comment. There had to be some deep-seated rationale, I thought. And then it struck me like a lightning bolt: their lack of interest in visiting Washington DC is due to their lack of curiosity.

A while back I was having lunch with a friend of mine in London, England. He is a true Londoner; born, raised and lives in London.

As we were chatting over lunch, he said to me, "I have friends in Oshkosh." I replied, "Oshkosh, Wisconsin?" and he said, "Yes, Oshkosh, Wisconsin." Nothing against Oshkosh, but I found it interesting that someone from London would have friends in a moderately obscure town in Wisconsin. As we were talking, he said to me, "You know, people in Oshkosh are more concerned with Mrs. Jones's cat that's up a tree than they are with what's going on in the world. They lack"—he paused, searching for another word—"they lack…" and I interjected, "Curiosity?" "Yes," he said. "They lack curiosity."

Markets are changing so fast along with technology and customer demands that you must have a high curiosity factor if you are to identify customer problems and learn new ways to produce better results for your stakeholders. Curiosity may not have killed the cat, but a lack of curiosity can kill your career.

Curiosity helps you in:

- *Building customer relationships.* People are drawn to those who show interest in them. Having an abiding fascination in others gives you the opportunity to learn new things about them, thereby making a deeper connection.
- *Increasing your business acumen.* Being curious about your own industry and the industries of your stakeholders drives you to learn more. As you satisfy your curiosity, you're augmenting your ability to add value to your customers' business.
- *Solving customer problems.* Customers want solutions for the challenges they face. It's only possible to create a mean-

85

ingful solution if you're motivated by true curiosity about what's actually going on and why those problems occur.

- *Motivating your employees.* Some bosses think of employees as cogs in a corporate machine. However, if you want to get the best out of people, you must be curious about their dreams and desires. What do they want to achieve? If you are not curious enough to know the answer to that question, you are missing great opportunities to help them to be more successful in their careers and in their lives.

Curiosity allows you to create new, greater value for stakeholders. A common trait of nearly every successful professional is unhesitant curiosity. This includes curiosity about their business, their employees, and their stakeholders. Today's professionals need a high curiosity level along with acute listening skills to identify problems and learn new ways to create competitive business and market advantage.

That may seem intuitive, but Gino's research shows that we often prefer to talk rather than to listen with curiosity. For instance, when she asked some 230 high-level leaders in executive education classes what they would do if confronted with an organizational crisis stemming from both financial and cultural issues, most said they would take action: move to stop the financial bleeding and introduce initiatives to refresh the culture. Only a few said they would ask questions rather than simply impose their ideas on others.

Management books commonly encourage leaders assuming new positions to communicate their vision from the start rather than ask employees how they can be most helpful. That's bad advice. Such fears and beliefs are misplaced, Gino's research shows. When we demonstrate curiosity about others by asking questions, people like us *more* and view us as *more* competent, and the heightened trust makes our relationships more interesting and intimate. By asking questions, we promote more meaningful connections and more creative outcomes.[24]

---

[24] "The Business Case for Creativity." HRB Harvard Business Review. September–October 2018.

YOUR SECRET WEAPON

The inspiration for the Polaroid instant camera was a three-year-old's question. Inventor Edwin Land's daughter was impatient to see a photo her father had just snapped. When he explained that the film had to be processed, she wondered aloud, "Why do we have to wait for the picture?"

In 2000 when Greg Dyke had been named director general of the BBC but hadn't yet assumed the position, he spent five months visiting the BBC's major locations, assembling the staff at each stop. Employees expected a long presentation but instead got a simple question: "What is the one thing I should do to make things better for you?" Dyke would listen carefully and then ask, "What is the one thing I should do to make things better for our viewers and listeners?" By asking questions and genuinely listening to the responses, Dyke modeled the importance of those behaviors. He also highlighted the fact that when we are exploring new terrain, listening is as important as talking: It helps us fill gaps in our knowledge and identify other questions to investigate.

During our school years, we are taught to find the right answers, not to find the best questions. This also applies to leadership, where asking questions is sometimes perceived as an act of vulnerability—or even a sign of "weak" leadership. Often the opposite is true—being genuinely curious will help you to be a better leader. Why? Because asking questions keeps you in a learning rather than judgment mode; it keeps you focused on the bigger picture and thus will help to find better solutions. As Eric Schmidt, Google's CEO from 2001 to 2011, has said, "We run this company on questions, not answers."[25]

If it is creativity and original thinking we seek, then we must force a change in our perspective. Staying inside the box means accepting the status quo. We don't change our perspective by maintaining the status quo. One way to step outside your comfort zone is to do something different in your life. Better yet, do something you really don't want to do. I'm not talking about taking out the trash. I am referring to how breakthrough moments can happen when you

---

[25] "Why Curiosity Matters." Ms Francesca Gino. Harvard Business Review. September–October 2018.

are curious about the potential outcome of doing something you really do not want to do. Here is a personal case in point.

I was asked by an acquaintance of mine to speak to the Publicity Club of Los Angeles at their monthly meeting. I really didn't want to do it as I had an early flight the next morning from Los Angeles to Naples, Florida, as part of a retreat in Captiva Island, Florida, for the Atlanta office partners of the law firm of Paul Hastings Janofsky & Walker, LLP. I tried to come up with a compelling reason not to be available for this engagement, but I couldn't. Plus, I was curious to know the response my remarks would generate, as I had not presented to any audiences regarding my work at that time. I agreed to speak on that fateful Monday evening. Why fateful? Because as I was bombing in my presentation, the United States—under General Norman Schwarzkopf—began its bombing mission in Iraq.

About four or five months later, my acquaintance from the Publicity Club phoned me to say that a lawyer from Birmingham, England was coming to the United States to look at best practices among law firm practice development. He was going to meet with law firms in San Francisco and Los Angeles. At that time, I was director of client development for Paul Hastings, Janofsky & Walker, which was headquartered in Los Angeles. I agreed to meet with Adrian D. Bland, partner of the then law firm of Evershed Wells & Hind, which today is the international law firm known as Eversheds Sutherland.

Following Adrian's meeting with other US law firms, he contacted me to say that we were doing things that other law firms were not doing in client development. I responded that I was not surprised to hear that as I had the scars on my back to prove it to be true. We were performing breakthrough programming foreign to most law firms: marketing! I was asked to come to Birmingham and spend time discussing law-firm marketing and client-service programming with Evershed Wells & Hind partners. I did and that started a seven-year consulting relationship with *Eversheds* that was a springboard to my international consulting business.

Since that initial meeting in Birmingham, I have worked for some of the top law firms and other clients in Australia, North America, the United Kingdom, and Europe. Not only has the work

YOUR SECRET WEAPON

been rewarding, I have had the opportunity to meet and become friends with many of my clients. The beauty of this experience is having been able to have my wife, Joy, and our daughter, Kathleen, accompany me on several international client-work-related trips.

Would Joy, Kathleen, and I have attended a performance of *The Phantom* in London, or Kathleen and I attend a performance of *Tosca* at the Vienna opera house, or she and I see the Hungarian crown jewels at the House of Parliament in Budapest? Probably not! How many fathers get the opportunity to spend a day with their daughter in Toledo, Spain, one of the most unique cities on the planet? My sense is, not many.

These rewarding experiences are the by-product of my business that was launched following a presentation to the Los Angeles Publicity Club that I didn't want to make. My message here is clear: do something you really don't want to do. You might be pleasantly surprised by the results.

When defining your success, remember this important thing: success is a journey that contains multiple peaks and valleys. One success builds on another. A setback can be your greatest learning experience. Setbacks and mistakes will also help you build your success. I find value in an unofficial US Marine Corps slogan: *Improvise, Adapt, Overcome.* Isn't that what we really do in our daily lives and our careers?

The coronavirus disease (COVID-19) has caused the world to seriously improvise, adapt in an effort to overcome this deadly pandemic. When roadblocks stymie our personal lives, jobs, or career goals, we have to overcome these obstacles. Those who are unable to adapt to these challenges can experience serious personal, business, and career setbacks. And we must improvise solutions to these challenges. Out of this improvisation comes action steps needed to not only compete but to survive in today's ever-changing world.

An example of the capacity to improvise, adapt, and overcome can be found in a person whose name you probably recognize: Walt Disney. I'm a huge Disney fan. After graduate school, I worked part-time in security at Disneyland, and our daughter was a part-time Walt Disney World cast member for ten years.

When Walt Disney was a young man, he was hired to work at *The Kansas City Star* newspaper. He was later fired from that newspaper because of—are you ready for this?—lack of *creativity*. Walt Disney overcame a career setback. He adapted, and he also improvised. Years later, the Walt Disney Company bought ABC broadcasting which owned *The Kansas City Star*. How strange that he was fired because he was not creative enough, and yet his company was creative enough to own that newspaper.

"If you want to write creatively, you need to think creatively. To think creatively, do something different in your life." Those were the words of Ms. Peggy White, who was the professor in my creative writing class at UCLA. That sounded like useful information, but what was I going to do about it? What could I do that would inspire me to be creative? After a few moments of introspection, I came up with an activity that would challenge my behavior. I would ride around in a city bus in South Central Los Angeles at midnight. That would take me out of my comfort zone. I had never done that before. So I did it. If I ever do that again, I will be heavily armed. Everyone else was!

While its social and economic conditions have improved, South-Central Los Angeles was a pretty rough area in the 1970s. Riding around in the middle of the night in a city bus made me think of little things I had taken for granted. I never had to wait for transportation to get where I want to go. I had my own car. Safety was not something I had given much thought. I thought about it that night. As the only white person on the bus, I felt more than a little out of place. Such were the feelings I had never experienced before. These unique feelings can be a resource to call upon when seeking to free our creative spirit.

More and more in our fast-moving global economy, we are becoming ever more reliant on the inventiveness of ordinary, unique human beings. We are in desperate need of people who are knowledgeable, capable, dynamic, and inventive. More and more we need to be able to expand our creative spirit. That means teaching ourselves to see things backward, inside out, and upside down. It means looking for solutions to problems from another perspective entirely.

YOUR SECRET WEAPON

We can achieve that by looking at problems, situations, and opportunities from different vantage points.

Therefore, we should constantly ask:

"Why is this so?"
"What makes it different?'
"When did it happen?"
"What difference will it make?"
"Who will benefit from this?"

Creativity should be encouraged and highly prized. It is the key to our success and our future. All new ideas need nurturing and support, so we must support and respect others when they come up with a new idea. Is there a better way to think beyond the boundaries what is conventionally accepted? Strangely enough, when you start to think outside the box, the box simply goes away.

I have had the pleasure to know two geniuses whose creativity drove them to achieve extraordinary business success. One is Dr. An Wang, founder of Wang Laboratories, for whom I worked. A Chinese-American computer engineer and inventor, Dr. Wang, the holder of forty patents and twenty-three honorary degrees, built Wang Laboratories from a one-man electrical fixtures store on top of a Boston garage into one of the world's major computer manufacturers.

From an entity with only $600, no orders, no contracts, and no office furniture, Wang Laboratories grew into a corporation employing more than thirty thousand people. The company became a market leader in desktop calculators and also achieved success with word processors. Dr. Wang was one of the most celebrated engineers and entrepreneurs of the twentieth century.

"I don't know how many countless thousands of thousands of people owe a debt of gratitude for what he did," Gov. Michael S. Dukakis once said of Dr. Wang. He was one of only sixty-nine members of the National Inventors Hall of Fame at the time of his death in 1990.[26]

Jack Ryan was the other genius I have known. His name is not well known, but his brilliant work is. While he helped design the Sparrow and Hawk guided missile systems during his time at Raytheon, his creative brilliance became known by creating some of the most prolific toys in the world. While at Mattel Corporation, Ryan created the design and patented the Barbie doll. Since the launch of Mattel's Barbie fashion doll in 1959, Barbie has become a cultural icon in America and around the world, generating sales well in excess of $3 billion.

The commercial success of Barbie has allowed Mattel to become the ninth most valuable toy brand worldwide as of 2018. Ryan also created the popular Hot Wheels and Chatty Cathy. Jack Ryan held over one thousand patents at the time of his death in 1991. For both of these people, key elements in driving their professional successes was their ability to be both curious and creative.

---

[26] *New York Times.* March 25, 1990, Section 1, Page 3.

CHAPTER 7

Mission

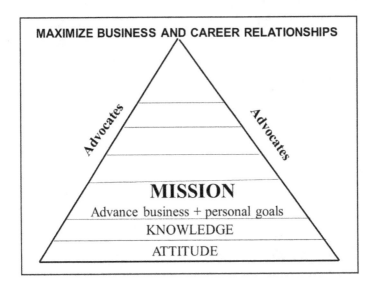

Building upon the previous chapter highlighting the importance of knowledge, the next step along our path to turning stakeholders into valued advocates requires us to fully understand the advocate candidate's mission. When you know your stakeholder's mission, you hold the key to unlocking what matters most to him or her.

The ability to connect at the higher level that we want to achieve with targeted stakeholders requires that you establish common ground to more thoroughly understand the other person. This is particularly true early on in your relationship. Let's examine common ground.

There are four conversational topics that most people will relate to. It's important that you find something you sincerely like about your stakeholder, something you genuinely have in common. These are not obtrusive subjects; rather they demonstrate an honest interest based on focused listening in what they have to say. Now you are on your way to creating a meaningful bond with your stakeholder.

These conversational topics are:

Family

- People love to talk about their family. If you can establish dialogue that allows your stakeholder to relate to you with family experiences similar to yours, this is the strongest common bond topic of conversation. Children are the ultimate common bond topic. If you have children of similar ages, chances are you have similar experiences you can discuss.

Occupation

- Once you know what they do for a living, ask them why they chose that career path. Ask them what they like best about their work; what are some of their biggest challenges they face at work? Get them to expand on their responses by demonstrating that you are genuinely interested in what they have to say.

Recreation

- Talk with them about their hobbies and interests, sports, vacations, and similar topics. Ask what they like to do when not at work. People enjoy talking about their vacations. Ask them what they do when they take a vacation.

Motivation

- Any time someone will talk to you about their dreams and future plans, you are on the correct path to cementing common ground. Ask them, "When your feet hit the floor in the morning, what drives you to be successful?"

How do you identify people who can become your advocate? Your potential advocate is someone who is committed to helping you succeed. The advocate possesses two important values: (1) they *want* to see you succeed, and (2) they are *committed* to helping you succeed. But this is only possible when built upon a mutual relationship.

Showing real interest in what is important to other people is vital for building effective relationships. Show them that you are committed to their success. Likewise, your target advocate must understand your mission in order to help you achieve your goals. This is a truly mutual admiration synergy between the two of you. If you aren't asked, make clear what your goals are.

To achieve the overall objective of taking relationships to the desired higher and more-meaningful level, you need to understand what they want to achieve. You must understand your stakeholder's mission. If we don't know what your stakeholder wants to achieve in his or her career, it is nearly impossible to create the unprecedented value that is required to take relations to the high ground of being an advocate.

Knowing how to help the stakeholder achieve these objectives produces the kind of utility that your stakeholder will value. For example, can you introduce your stakeholders to influential people and deal makers? How about providing unique information valuable to his or her business or personal cause? Being available to them when they call upon you are ways to endear yourself to your prospective advocate.

Now is the time to create that road map. Now is the time to dive into your stakeholder's mission. I don't believe you can demonstrate to your stakeholders that you are committed to their success without understanding their mission. Remember, when you understand someone's mission, you hold the key to opening the door to that which matters the most to them. We begin to understand their mission by examining © *The Advocate Profile.*

Your goal is to connect and/or to reconnect on a more-refined manner with your target advocate. Use the following questionnaire to develop a profile of your target advocate. Some of your resources for the information might include the target person, select members of your personal network, trade publications, secretaries, receptionists, suppliers, newspapers, assistants, and the Internet. Continue to expand your knowledge of this person both professionally and personally. You'll find topics for opening conversations, which can open doors for your target advocate and for yourself.

1. Name:
2. Employer:
3. Home address:
4. Birth date:
5. Name of high school:
6. Name of college:
7. Degree(s) received:
8. Fraternity/sorority:
9. Sports interests:
10. Spouse's name and occupation:
11. Spouse's education:
12. Spouse's interests:
13. Anniversary date:
14. Children, if any, names and ages:
15. Children's education:
16. Previous employment (most recent first):
    a. Company/Firm:
    b. Location:
    c. Title:
    d. Dates:
17. Professional memberships:
18. Offices held/Honors:
19. Clubs, fraternal associations, or service clubs:
20. Politically active? Party?
21. Religion:
22. Highly sensitive/confidential items *not* to be discussed with this person (i.e., divorce, etc.):

YOUR SECRET WEAPON

23. On what subjects outside of business does this person have strong feelings?

I cannot emphasize enough the importance and the value to you and to your targeted advocate of knowing the answer to one very important question. This is a question you are not likely to ask the first time you meet someone. You ask this question *after* you have obtained much of the information of 1–23 above.

The mere fact that you ask this question of a potential advocate will separate you from the vast majority with whom you compete in today's business world because your competition is not likely to think of this question, let alone to ask it. Knowing the answer to this question will serve as a focus for the activities you will take to turn this person into your advocate: *How does this person want to be remembered when he/she ends his/her career?*

Is there a more-important question to ask someone that you want to turn into an advocate? I think not. This question helps you identify the action steps for taking your relationship with that individual to the desired level of being an advocate. You identify those action steps by knowing the answers to the following questions.

24. Who does this person want to meet to advance his business and /or his personal interests?
25. What can you do to make this happen?
26. What is this person's immediate business objective?
27. What can you do to help him/her achieve that objective?
28. What is his/her long-range business objective?
29. What can you do to help him/her achieve that objective?
30. Where does this person want his/her career to be in three years?
31. What can you do to help him/her achieve that career objective?

Your stakeholder knows how he or she wants to be remembered. What they have likely not done is share that information with you. When they do, you have a unique opportunity to help them craft their legacy.

CHAPTER 8

Value-Focused

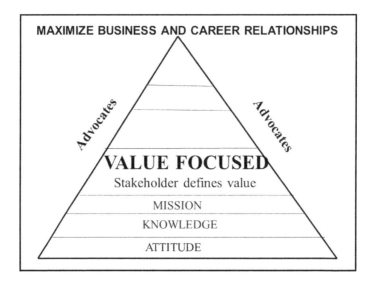

Once we understand our stakeholder's mission—what he or she wants to achieve in his/her career—we can turn our attention to creating unprecedented value in our stakeholder relationships. To do so, it is important to have a mutual exchange of value equal to or greater than the value you receive from the other person. To get what you want from your stakeholders, give them greater value than they give you. This will eventually pay substantial benefit to you.

The utility you confer to someone depends on the individual. So please keep this in mind: I don't determine the value I bring to my stakeholders. You don't determine the value you bring to your stakeholders. Our stakeholders determine the value we offer them. How does your stakeholder define your value? What is the value you bring to your stakeholder? Are you highly valued by those who are important to your success? You need to know the answer to those questions. How do you do that? Ask them!

The pursuit of a cup of coffee can shed light on how value can be perceived. While on my way to the local Starbuck's in Orlando to get my grande nonfat latte, I noticed a young man standing on the corner, holding a sign that read: "Trying to get to Jacksonville, any little bit will help." If he really needs to get to Jacksonville and he doesn't have the money for bus fare and I give him $20, his perception of that money is probably highly favorable. Now I have some friends who live in a very excusive community in the Orlando area. If I give some of my friends there $20, it won't even get their attention. They are likely thinking that they can buy a couple of golf balls with it. The fact is that a $20 bill is a $20 bill. The reality is how that $20 is valued.

Here are three utility principles to keep in mind:

- Value is determined not by the price of something but by the utility it yields.
- Utility is the subjective benefit that a person experiences.
- The utility you confer to someone depends on the needs of that individual.

Let's take value one step further by looking at four value issues important for turning stakeholders into prized advocates.

Interest and Attention

When you demonstrate a high level of interest and attention to your stakeholders and customers, they are more inclined to support you. This is not because of a good bargain or because of price differential. Customers return and stakeholders support you because of the way you make them feel. Generally speaking, people will forget what you said, and people will forget what you did. People are not likely to forget how you made them feel. Everyone who can have an impact on your business and your career wants to feel important at some point in their life. Make your stakeholders and your customers feel important.

One company that understands the utility of making your stakeholders feel important is the Hallmark company. In fact, it is specifically written into their company engagement philosophy:

Your customers want to feel good about being your customer. It's about engagement, a two-way interaction that's both meaningful and personal. Genuine connection happens when your customers feel like they matter to you in ways that go beyond goods and services; when they feel like an individual and not a data blip. So when you're looking for the best acquisition strategy, go for advocacy. When your customers become advocates for your brand, you can count on them for creating your new customers.[27]

Do not underestimate the power of small things because the small things add up to make a big difference. A company that understands this is the grocery chain, Publix. As the largest employee-owned retail grocery chain in the United States, Publix Super Markets owns 11 percent of the supermarket business in Florida. Taking the seemingly mundane task of grocery shopping to a new level, Publix has made the exceptional customer experience second to none among supermarkets.

Focusing on their attention to detail, Publix does small actions to make its customers want to return. For example, the cashiers do not stand behind the cash register when they are not making a transaction. Instead, they stand in front of their "station," greeting each customer and offering assistance. Customers rarely bags their own groceries; instead they are greeted with an eager employee willing to help. All employees wear a button exclaiming, "No tipping please," because the company believes that great customer service is given to all customers.

When I have asked Publix for a special order, they ask if I would like them to phone me when it comes in. When I asked an employee

---

[27] http://www.hallmarkbusinessconnections.com/customer-engagement

YOUR SECRET WEAPON

at one of Publix's competitors, located three hundred yards away, where certain items are located, the employee points to the location. When I ask at Publix, an employee walks with me to show me where that item is located. Publix creates an atmosphere for customers to become repeat customers. Their company slogan is, "Where shopping is a pleasure." Creating an emotional connection is simply good business. Oh, by the way, the Publix competitor located three hundred yards away went out of business several years ago.

As a case in point, all you have to do is look at the jewelry industry.

> The industry hasn't exactly had an easy time wooing millennials, and winning the hearts of their younger siblings in Generation Z may prove even trickier. Jewelers are increasingly looking at how to do that, as evidenced by a new report on the post-millennial generation produced for CIBJO, the World Jewelry Confederation. Report author Jonathan Kendall said Gen Z shoppers—who already spend an estimated $163 billion a year—rank the environment as their No. 1 concern, and some 70% consider sustainability before they make a purchase. They also value authenticity, transparency, diversity, and a personal touch. Plus, they are tough customers. "The more added value, the better," Kendall said. "That can come from its environmental credentials or its social value."[28]

Value is defined broadly beyond just the product itself. Consumers are buying more than a product; rather they are buying the brand in its entirety—its mission, ethos, and impact.

What are these potential jewelry customers seeking when they identify diversity, a "personal touch," and more value added that can

---

[28] https://www.jckonline.com/magazine-article/november-december-2019

come from a company's environmental or its social value? They want more than the perceived utility that jewelry purchases generate. They seek an emotional connection not just with the product they purchased; they want an emotional connection from whom they purchased that product.

Responsiveness

When your stakeholder needs you, be there for him or her. How accessible are you for your stakeholder? Do you respond to your stakeholder in an expeditious manner? When you meet with a stakeholder are you always on time? Here's a novel idea: How about developing a reputation for being early to stakeholder events? I have heard plenty of people provide excuses why they were late to a meeting. I have yet to hear anyone apologize for arriving early for an event. I am waiting to hear someone say, "Gee, I am sorry for arriving ten minutes early. The traffic moved much faster than I anticipated."

Trust and Confidence

If we can agree that *trust* is at the center of an advocate relationship, then isn't it important to know how much the other person trusts you? Do you believe the other person values your knowledge and your input? You need to know the answer to that question. Continue to enhance the trust your stakeholders have by doing great work for them. Seek their input on how you can improve the service you provide stakeholders.

Value of services rendered for fees paid

If you provide a stakeholder a service that he or she pays you for, ask them if they believe the fees you charge are competitive with other qualified providers of similar services. Ask if they believe you are good value for the money they pay you.

According to *Forbes* magazine November 2019, executives recognize the importance of meeting customer expectations and make

YOUR SECRET WEAPON

it one of the top pillars of growth. But they incorrectly estimate customer expectations by largely aiming to meet customer expectations by reacting rather than anticipating those needs. Accurately anticipating customer needs offers individuals and organizations opportunities to create unparalleled stakeholder value.[29]

The same is true for our stakeholder relations. When it comes to creating exceptional stakeholder value, there is a vast difference between your stakeholders' *expressed needs* and their *unexpressed wishes*. When you recognize the difference between the two, you position yourself to not only create extraordinary stakeholder value; you separate yourself from your competition.

"Expressed needs" are communicated in various ways: an advertisement seeking employee candidates; written statements of vision, purpose, and values; request for proposals (RFPs); performance reviews—all can communicate what is expected of you. Job/position descriptions also communicate what is expected of an employee. Keep in mind that job descriptions do not specify every task an employee could do to support an organization. Going "above and beyond" should be a goal of each person who wants to achieve more in his/her career. It's much easier to achieve more in your career if you understand what is not written but is highly valued by your employer and stakeholders.

For marketing and sales professionals, remember that any professional who is motivated, who has good product/service knowledge, and who can conduct an effective customer or prospect needs interview can identify expressed needs. That does not separate you from the competition. That just gets you in the door to compete. Your challenge is to determine your stakeholders' unexpressed wishes.

The Ritz-Carlton Hotel Company, LLC, which operates five-star resorts and luxury hotels worldwide, has received all the major awards the hospitality industry and leading consumer organizations can bestow. Ritz-Carlton is the first and only hotel company twice honored with the Malcolm Baldrige National Quality Award from the United States Department of Commerce.

---

[29] Forbes Insights. *Forbes Magazine*. Issue November 2019.

Jon McGavin is the general manager of The Ritz-Carlton Orlando, Grande Lakes, one of the most successful of the Ritz Carlton properties. In this position he oversees operations of the hotel, which includes 582 guest rooms, a 40,000-square-foot spa, over 110,000 square feet of indoor and outdoor meeting space, and an eighteen-hole championship golf course. A veteran of the hospitality industry, McGavin, has been with Marriott International for over thirty years. He shared with me some of the characteristics that help make the Ritz-Carlton so unique.

"What we are looking for are loyal guests," McGavin points out. "A guest staying one time where we take his money and he never wants to come back again does no good. I look at a guest as an investment. Every guest is worth hundreds of thousands of dollars to our organization. We want them to become loyal to this organization."[30]

Employees who are strongly connected to your company through a set of positive emotional experiences will express that positive experience to others. The employee experience should be treated as an emotionally engaging journey that starts from the hiring process, onboarding, anniversary celebrations, community-service commitments, recognition programs, and every aspect of the employee's journey.

Ritz-Carlton takes great pride in the mystique it creates. Part of the Ritz-Carlton mystique is the fulfillment of unexpressed wishes and needs, and they are very specific in how to accomplish that objective. The goal is to develop such strong emotional engagement between the hotel's staff and their guests that a guest will not consider staying anywhere else, if they have an option. Ritz-Carlton understands that relationships precede financial results and instead rely on a robust data set that demonstrates the impact that engaged employees and repeat customers have on the bottom line.

How do you find the unexpressed wishes? They are not on some plaque or some inspirational credo. Stakeholders hold these wishes inside of them in their hearts and in their dreams of what they need, what they want to do, and what they want to accomplish. The

---

[30] Jon McGavin Interview with Byron G. Sabol. Orlando, Florida. May 2017.

YOUR SECRET WEAPON

Ritz-Carlton understands the importance of unexpressed wishes as explained in one of their service values: *The Ritz-Carlton experience enlivens the senses, instills well-being, and fulfills even the unexpressed wishes and needs of our guests.*

Sometimes customers express their needs, but often you need to look beyond their words to discover what they actually need. In other words, their expressed need is not the full truth, and a good customer service professional is able to dig deeper and unearth the actual unexpressed need.

The Ritz-Carlton commitment to understanding expressed needs and unexpressed wishes is apparent in the following from the Ritz-Carlton Leadership Center. One of the service values at The Ritz-Carlton is, I am always responsive to the expressed and unexpressed wishes and needs of our guests. In order to detect the unexpressed needs of your customers, you need to look for clues and have your "radar on and antenna up." Here are two classic Ritz-Carlton examples of recognizing unexpressed needs:

A guest asks: "What kind of scotch do you have?"

When guests ask a server for a particular brand of alcohol, they're saying, "I like it. I want some. Serve it to me." However, when they ask what kinds of alcohol, desserts, or anything else are available, they are saying, "I'm open. Take me on an adventure. Turn me on to something new." This gives the server an opportunity to create a special memory. If the server hands a menu to the customer and walks away, then the server is missing an opportunity to connect and engage with customers.

If the server tells a story about the scotch and turns the customer on to something new, then the server not only answers the customer's question but also creates a lasting memory. A server at The Ritz-Carlton learned about a guest's interest in modern rice wines and sake. The server was able to track down the specific sake the guest was looking for and had a bottle of it sent to her home.

A guest asks: "Is it raining?"

It is clearly pouring outside. The guest can see the rain—so you know that the guest is not looking for a "yes" or "no" answer. The guest's question is straightforward, but your answer should uncover what the real need is. Does the guest want to know how long it is expected to rain? Is the guest concerned about the rain postponing an upcoming event? Does the guest need an umbrella or a taxi in order to stay dry? By finding out the guest's true needs, you can show genuine care.

A guest asks: "Do you have laundry/dry cleaning service?"

The guest may want to use a cleaning service at some point in his or her stay. However, this question may also indicate a "clothing crisis." Clothing can be an issue for guests, and sometimes clothing can be an embarrassing situation. Guests can be reluctant to admit that they've stained their only tie or ripped their shirt. It's important to approach questions regarding attire with compassion and kindness. Oftentimes guests are panicked because they have an important event or meeting to attend.

When a frequent business guest checked in to The Ritz-Carlton, Shanghai, at 1:00 a.m., the front desk agent noticed the guest was anxious and was wearing casual shorts. Because the front desk agent was alert to these clues, he was able to discover the guest's unexpressed need. The guest's suit pants had been torn, and he needed pants for an important meeting at 10:00 a.m. the next day. The front desk agent woke up early, found a store, and delivered the new pants to the guest in time for the meeting.[31]

Creativity has a prominent place in the Ritz culture. "When I think of creativity, I think of personalized service," McGavin points out. "Our guests don't walk around with a big sign around their neck saying 'vacation,' 'honeymoon,' 'wedding,' 'golf trip,' or 'spa trip with the girls.' People don't walk in with a badge telling us what mood they are in.

"Here is an example of what I am talking about regarding the creative element. We have a couple of artists on our guest relations team, and we had a family staying with us. The father, unfortunately, had late stage cancer and was in a tough spot. But one of our guest relations agents took a portrait of the family, sketched it, and framed

---

[31] The Ritz-Carlton Leadership Center. (http://ritzcarltonleadershipcenter.com/2016/01/recognnizing-unexpressed-needs)

YOUR SECRET WEAPON

it for them. And you know that is not something that is scripted. That is not something where we say, if you have a family where a father or a mother is going to pass away, you do this. Our artist did this on his own. He used his initiative and his creativity to make their days just a little bit more memorable."

Identifying and acting on your stakeholders' unexpressed wishes cannot only add extraordinary value to that person; you separate yourself from the pact. You have an opportunity to cut through the veneer of relationships—to stand out from your competition. Identify unexpressed wishes and look into your stakeholder's heart. Here is an example of what I am talking about:

The evening of April 12, 2014, in Dallas, my wife and I had the pleasure to meet former President George W. Bush and to speak briefly with him. A photo of President Bush with my wife and me hangs proudly in our residence. Later that evening Mr. Bush was speaking to a group of about four hundred executives, and the subject came up about how Mr. Bush was trying to get to know Russian President Vladimir Putin better. The two were discussing a religious cross that was given to Mr. Putin by Mr. Putin's mother. Mr. Putin, President Bush pointed out to the audience, had lost that cross, and it was important for him to find it.

When Mr. Putin was describing his deep concern to find that cross, President Bush said to the audience, "I looked in his eyes, and I saw his soul." I thought that was a remarkable comment. You see, sometimes we need to look inside our advocate candidate's soul to find out who they are and what drives them. When we do that, we uncover deep-seated information that allows us to relate with the other person at our desired higher, more-meaningful level.

The following sums up this point: I had thought for some time that a client of mine was a potential advocate for me. I also sensed he wanted to be chairman of one of the largest firms in the legal profession. He never said that to me; I just sensed it. So I told him directly, "You can become chairman of this firm."

He said he didn't think so because he said that he didn't have the management skills to be chairman. So I said, "How can I help you?" After thinking about it for a while, he asked me to put together

107

a list of top business schools in the United States that offered short courses—two or three-week programs. I did, and he subsequently attended Harvard Business School and Wharton Business School.

This man became one of three finalists to become chairman of that firm. For unrelated personal reasons, he withdrew from the election process. Had he stayed the course, I am convinced he would have been selected chairman of that firm.

Here's my point. My client didn't come to me and ask, "Hey, Byron, I'm thinking about running to be chairman of our firm, can you help me?" I had a feeling that was something he would want to do in his career. Be sensitive and be aware of what you believe your target advocates want to achieve. Know what they want to do with their careers. Collaborate with them.

Revisit questions 24–31 of ©*The Advocate Profile.* Allow me to repeat that you must know the answer to the all-important question: *How does this person want to be remembered when he/she ends his/ her career?* Look them in the eye and find their soul. Identify their unexpressed wishes and take action on them! Make the all-important emotional connection with your stakeholders.

Superior performers focus on the outcomes, not the steps. The "wow" experience is the outcome. Focus on creating the "wow" for those individuals important to your business, career, and life success. Wows come in different sizes. Some wows are large; some wows are smaller. A "wow," by definition, makes a very favorable impression. So why wouldn't we want to make that impression on our stakeholders? Creating that "wow" experience is also one great way to make that emotional connection.

We all have opportunities to create the "wow" experience for others. I had been consulting for several years for a client in the United Kingdom. Because my work was well received, they reengaged me. For the first five years of my seven-plus-year relationship with this firm, our relationship was professional and cordial. There was no emotional connection.

One day I received a phone call from my client in Birmingham, United Kingdom, asking me to do them a favor. They informed me that one of the firm's clients was, unfortunately, suffering from terminal cancer. He was an avid Michael Jordan fan, and I was asked by my client if I could obtain a basketball signed by MJ—not one I could purchase at a collector store; one that had their client's name on the ball signed by Michael Jordan. I said, "Of course, no problem, I can do that." I hung up the phone and asked myself, "How am I am going to do that?" Michael Jordan doesn't know me. I have never met him.

I contacted some lawyer friends of mine in Chicago who represented Michael Jordan and got the ball signed and delivered to my client in the United Kingdom. Both my client and their client were thrilled with the result. While I didn't do anything exceptional, I was able to respond to an opportunity that resulted in a "wow" experience for my client and for their client. My connection with this firm started by doing good work, being reengaged, and then responding when they needed a simple task to be done for a most worthy cause.

Receiving that basketball was extraordinarily important to that cancer victim. When you can make even a small difference—like an autographed basketball—in someone's life, the rewards will come back to you. The "wow" experience had been created by an opportunity to get a basketball signed by an NBA legend. You make that difference when you create the "wow" experience for that other person.

Here's my thinking about requests from stakeholders: if a stakeholder of mine asks me to take action on his or her behalf and that action is not illegal, immoral, or will not hurt anyone in any way, I always respond with a "yes." I'll figure out later how to make it happen. This is another example of stepping outside of your comfort zone. Stretch a bit, and you will likely find favorable results.

CHAPTER 9

Advisor

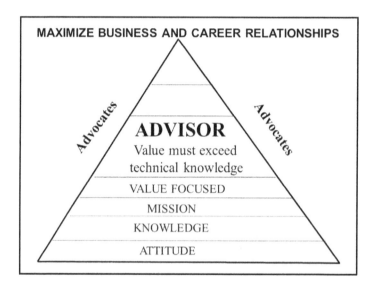

The next step along our systematic method of connecting at the desired highest level is the advisor. Connecting at the desired high level means seeing yourself as an advisor to your select stakeholders and others who are important to you. To be an advisor to your stakeholders requires that you bring value that exceeds your technical knowledge.

Don't underestimate your capacity to serve as an advisor to the stakeholders you want to turn into advocates. You have knowledge and experience that are unique to you alone. You are educated in many ways. And I am not taking about university degrees. There

YOUR SECRET WEAPON

are many ways that knowledge is acquired, and experience is gained outside the classroom, such as travel, being a caretaker to a loved one, or volunteering in your community to serve others. Remember, my father never went beyond the fourth grade; yet he provided valued advice over the years to our family's business, customers, and vendors.

Your universe of expertise goes much beyond the body of knowledge required for your job. Your capacity to advise stakeholders is grounded in your knowledge, experience, and insights that can be of value to others. Don't underestimate the potential this holds for your stakeholders.

So how do you know when you are in that advisor role? You are an advisor when:

- People seek information from you because of your technical knowledge and experience. They see you as a valued resource.
- People seek information from you that may or may not anything to do with your technical expertise. They see you as approachable, and they value your opinion on a variety of subjects.
- People ask you questions on subjects they believe you are highly qualified to answer.
- You are asked for your opinion during formal meetings and during informal gatherings.
- You are included as part of a team on important decisions.

Are you experiencing these kinds of moments? Are you engaged in conversations where stakeholders seek your input? If so, you are an advisor to those individuals. If not, you are not in an advisory role, and you are missing opportunities for developing advocates and elevating relationships to a higher level.

Too many professionals find themselves in the traditional customer-provider relationship. When you are seen as an advisor, you are no longer seen as the one providing a commodity. In fact, if you have the appropriate knowledge, effective communications skills, and confidence to deliver, then you can make yourself the go-to person sought after by your stakeholders. Do you want to be in a more-meaningful and more-enjoyable role in the workplace? Do you want to be more financially rewarded? Do you want to be someone who is sought out for your opinion and knowledge on important issues at work? Be that advisor and enjoy the advantages it offers.

CHAPTER 10

Personal

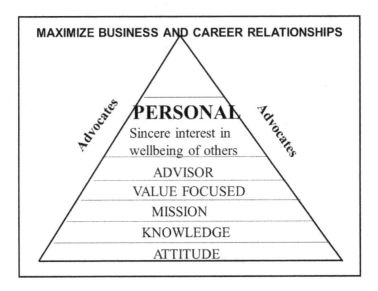

As you move from Attitude to Advisor in our pyramid, you will have laid the foundation for a highly rewarding personal relationship based on honesty, value, and trust with your prospective advocates. You have a personal relationship when the following criteria are met:

- You mutually understand that your relationship is all about the other person and not about you.
- You have taken the time to provide something that is highly valued by the other person not because you are expected to but simply because you can.

- Individuals confide in you. People will share information with you they are reluctant to share with others.
- They will tell you the truth—something you may or may not want to hear.
- They have confidence that you will be open to what the other person has to say.
- They know you will not be judgmental.
- They believe you will proactively listen to their comments and any of their concerns.
- They trust your judgment.
- You can be candid with each other.
- You talk about interests other than work.
- You are asked to attend client and stakeholder events.
- Each of you seeks opportunities to advance the other person's career and business interests.
- They know your goals and are initiating favorable communication on your behalf.
- They do not hesitate to ask you to take action on their behalf.
- They want to see you socially.
- You share a mutual admiration for each other.

CHAPTER 11

Emotion

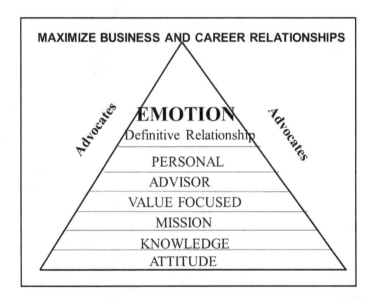

I used to think I was a decent athlete until I started playing golf, which I took up later in my life. Let me be more precise: I should have started playing golf when I was six rather than in my sixties. Golf is a sport that can humble you in a heartbeat. Watching the best professionals in the world play this game makes me appreciate just how skilled these athletes are. There is a special golf tournament experience I want to call to your attention: The Phoenix Open played at TCP Scottsdale.

On the first day of this tournament in 2013, Hall of Fame golfer Phil Michelson pointed his putter at the cup and started to walk toward the hole, ready to celebrate golf's magic number. Right at the end, though, the ball caught the right edge of the cup, curled 180 degrees to the other side of the hole, and stayed out. A fraction of an inch turned cheers to gasps and cost him a score of 59 in the first round of the tournament.

"Six feet to go, it was in the center," Mickelson said. "Three feet to go, it was in the center. A foot to go, it was in the center, and even as it's approaching the hole, I couldn't envision which side of the hole it could possibly miss on, and it ended up somehow just dying off at the end, catching the lip." A total letdown.

Playing partners, Jason Dufner and Rickie Fowler, also watched in disbelief when the twenty-five-foot birdie putt lipped out.

"Unlucky," Dufner said. "He was walking it in."

"I thought it was in," Fowler said. "I was pulling for him."

Mickelson settled for an eleven under sixty, matching the tournament record he already shared with Grant Waite and Mark Calcavecchia.

"Well, sixty is awesome," Mickelson said. "Last time I shot sixty here in '05, I birdied like the last three or four holes just to do that, and I was ecstatic, and I'm ecstatic to shoot sixty." And then he made a profound statement when he said, "But there's a big difference between sixty and fifty-nine."[32]

So what does this golf experience mean to us? The answer lies in Phil Michelson's statement: "But there's a big difference between sixty and fifty-nine." Few among the best golfers on the planet can shoot sixty. Even fewer can shoot fifty-nine. The difference between the two scores is only one stroke. What a monumental difference that one stroke represents: tournament champion or both tournament champion *and* tournament record setter!

You can implement the first six of our seven steps for developing advocates and shoot a sixty. You nail a fifty-nine when you implement the seventh step by creating an emotional relationship with your advocate candidates. With a fifty-nine, you become unique to

---

[32] http://espn.go.com/golf/story/_/id/8902484/phil-mickelson-just-misses-59-pga-tour-phoenix-open

YOUR SECRET WEAPON

those who are important to your success, and you become special in your capacity to help your advocate candidate achieve his or her business and career objectives. Please remember this: *emotional connection is the ultimate measure of your relationship with others.* Let's take a look at our seventh and final step.

Emotions determine what clients and customers respond to, what they buy, who they buy from, and why they reengage you. Successful professionals create an extremely competitive advantage for themselves by connecting to their stakeholders on an emotional level.

One way to establish an emotional connection is by creating a unique and personalized experience with your stakeholders. The Ritz-Carlton wants to generate a personalized experience with its stakeholders. As the Ritz-Carlton's Jon McGavin so poignantly stated, "I look at a guest as an investment." You make your investment by finding ways to connect emotionally with targeted stakeholders. And how do you know when you have created that emotional nexus with your stakeholders? Here's the answer:

You have an emotional relationship when the other person seeks opportunities to advance your interests without asking you first. When other people ask you to take action on their behalf that will advance their career and business agenda, you have established an emotional connection. When you do not have to ask for introductions to advance your cause, because the other person knows your goals and is initiating communications on your behalf, your emotional relationship has been established.

Remember the "$10,000 Advocate Test" referenced in chapter 4? You have that emotional relationship when you receive the $10,000 you needed in two days! Make the emotional connection, and you have a valued resource that will help you achieve great things in your careers and in your personal life.

Think of your last interaction with a customer/client. Now ask yourself, of everything that went on in that interaction, what does your customer/client remember as something worth coming back again? Was it the product, the service process, or the price they paid? Unless you have a precise understanding of how that customer/client felt, you only have a small fraction of what really counts for the customer to return.

You want more than just having your stakeholder coming back. You want that person evangelizing for you. How your stakeholder feels about those interactions leaves a lasting emotional impression with that individual. If that emotional impression is highly favorable, and you repeat that level of emotion, you are creating an evangelizer for you.

How individuals feel about your products or services and how you treat them is often determined by their emotional relationship with not only the value of products or services you provide but also with the people who represent these products and services. Antonia Hock of The Ritz-Carlton Leadership Center points out that you hire for culture first. "Vocational skills can be taught and refined over time. Attitude, selflessness, compassion, positive outlook, work ethic, and heart for serving others are essential to create a powerful foundation for CX (customer experience), and those cannot be taught. Today there are many tools and approaches that allow companies to adopt a model of cultural fit during the hiring process, and great companies are deploying these solutions as part of their global approach to hiring and talent management."[33]

There are no limits on how emotion can be used to connect with another person or audience, advance a cause, sell an idea, or even bring people to tears. As the great Roman Orator, Cicero, so eloquently stated, *"If you wish to persuade me, you must think my thoughts, feel my feelings, and speak my words."* Former US senator John Edwards understood Cicero's words. He understood the power of emotions.

Prior to being elected US senator in 1998, Edwards became one of America's wealthiest trial lawyers by winning record jury verdicts and settlements in cases alleging that the botched treatment of women in labor and their deliveries caused infants to develop cerebral palsy, a brain disorder that causes motor function impairment and lifelong disability.

---

[33] "Culture Is the Key to Great Service" by Antonia Hock, The Ritz-Carlton Leadership Center. May 7, 2019.

YOUR SECRET WEAPON

In the courtroom, his skills and accomplishments made national headlines:

- *The New York Times* called him "an exceptionally talented lawyer, endowed with a prodigious work ethic."
- *USA Today* wrote that his "magic with jurors" and his "star qualities" in court made him "legendary."
- *The Washington Post* captured the sentiments of his opponents when it described their cardinal rule for going against John Edwards: "Never let him near a jury."

Edwards' trial summaries "routinely went beyond a recitation of his case to a heart-wrenching plea to jurors to listen to the unspoken voices of injured children," according to a comprehensive analysis of Edwards' legal career.[34]

The *Globe* cited an example of Edwards' oratorical skills from a medical malpractice trial in 1985. Edwards had alleged that a doctor and a hospital had been responsible for the cerebral palsy afflicting then-five-year-old Jennifer Campbell.

"I have to tell you right now—I didn't plan to talk about this—right now I feel her (Jennifer), I feel her presence," Edwards told the jury according to court records. "[Jennifer's] inside me, and she's talking to you… And this is what she says to you. She says, 'I don't ask for your pity. What I ask for is your strength. And I don't ask for your sympathy, but I do ask for your courage.'"

Edwards's emotional plea worked. Jennifer Campbell's family won a record jury verdict of $6.5 million against the hospital where the girl was born.

Please remember this: Emotion stimulates action. Emotion leads to achievement. If you doubt this, consider the following:

During a trial that made national headlines, Edwards pulled a newspaper out of his jacket and started to read, "There was a wonderful, wonderful thing written this past spring. It involved the death

---

[34] boston.com news (The Boston Globe) by Wendy Davis, Globe Correspondent. September 15, 2003.

of a young boy who shouldn't have died, and what he wrote was this: 'We have to gather around this family not because we understand what they're going through, but because—but because they have to know we share their pain. Our feelings—our terrible, terrible feelings—prove that we really all are part of the same family. Their loss was our loss. Their child was our child.'" When the jury came back with the $23 million verdict, ten of the twelve jurors were crying, recalled the judge who presided at the trial. Can we agree that creating an emotional relationship is extremely important for getting what you want?

PARTING THOUGHTS

As we close out this journey, here are a few parting thoughts:

- Positive emotions drive business and career success.
- Build an "A" team of individuals.
- Implement the *stakeholder profile.*
- Know your stakeholders' expressed needs and their unexpressed wishes.
- Apply the *four value issues for connecting emotionally.*
- Know what people are saying about you when you are not around.
- Create the "wow" experience.
- Make the all-important emotional connection with select stakeholders.

Considering the challenging experiences our society has endured in 2020, I believe the following will help put things in perspective. You'll be the judge of that. They go like this:

- Before you say an unkind word, think of those who cannot speak.
- Before you complain about the taste of your food, consider those who have nothing to eat.
- Should you find yourself complaining about your husband or your wife, think of those who are crying out for a companion.
- If you complain about life, please think of someone you know who went too soon to heaven.

- And when you are tired and complain about work, consider the unemployed, the disabled, and those who wish they had your job.
- And finally, when depressing thoughts seem to get you down, put a smile on your face and say, "Hey, I'm alive and still around!"

And finally, I refer to the late actor Roy Scheider, who starred in such major films as *The French Connection, Fosse, Jaws, and Jaws II*, among others major films.

In December 2004, while seeing a doctor for a routine examination, he was diagnosed with multiple myeloma. Ten months later, speaking about the experience on *The Today Show*, he said he considered himself to be lucky. "Every single day it's a miracle," he said. "Every day is a miracle. Everything looks much prettier."

Enjoy your miracles!

ABOUT THE AUTHOR

Byron G. Sabol is an author and professional speaker. His consulting career has included providing business generation and client-care services to corporations and professional service firms in Austria, Australia, Czech Republic, England, France, Germany, Greece, India, Republic of Ireland, The Netherlands, United States, and Wales. Byron has presented to audiences in three continents.

As executive vice president of PIPE, the largest promotional fund for the mechanical construction trades industry in North America, Byron received the Diogenes Award for Excellence in Consumer Education presented by the University of Southern California School of Business and the Sales and Marketing Executives Association of Southern California.

Byron has a bachelor's degree in marketing and an MBA in management with honors. He has been a part-time faculty member at five universities in California and Florida. Mr. Sabol is author of the popular book, *Taming the Beast: Success with Difficult People* (ByeCap Press).

Byron, a self-proclaimed Chicago White Sox and University of Notre Dame sports fanatic, lives with his wife, Joy, and their daughter Kathleen, in Scottsdale, Arizona.

Kathleen C. Sabol is a graduate of Saint Mary's College at Notre Dame, Indiana. She holds master's degrees from The George Washington University and the University of Florida. She is the founder and designer of mila + stevie, a handcrafted jewelry brand based in Scottsdale, Arizona. In addition to being an entrepreneur and writer, her other interests include singing, running, and volunteering in her community.

CPSIA information can be obtained
at www.ICGtesting.com
Printed in the USA
FSHW010648160921
84801FS